THE
UNWRITTEN
RULES OF WOMEN'S LEADERSHIP

Step into your power, write your own rules
and succeed in your career

HELEN APPLEBY

Dear Meg,
    You don't need to
read this to be a
badass !!

♡ Helen
x

Re think

Cover image by Dorothy Shi Studio, New York
Punch Cartoon © Punch Cartoon Library/TopFoto

Contents

For my dad, Andy Appleby (1942–2015), who always told me, 'Girls can do anything boys can do.'

Introduction

When I was a child, my dad told me that girls could do anything boys could do – and I believed him.

He said nothing about how challenging the pursuit of my career was going to be. Often I was the only woman in the room, and struggled to be seen and heard appropriately. Studies have shown that men interrupt twice as much as women in business, and that when they interrupt, it's more likely to be women they are interrupting.

My dad also never told me how torn I would feel every day between my professional role and my 'other job' as a mum, how I would feel as though I was leaving work too early and arriving home too late – even though I worked only ten minutes from home!

I guess he didn't know – because he was a man.

Even now in 2020, only around 5% of Fortune 100 CEOs are women. There are also more Fortune 1500 CEOs called David than there are women CEOs!

It seemed as if all I could do to climb the corporate ladder was work harder. I felt uncomfortable with 'self-promotion', and I thought that if I just kept my head down and did a good job, I'd get noticed. I put in more effort and delivered even better results, only to find that it didn't work like that. When the major global role that I coveted came along, I was excited – until somebody told me the post had already been filled by a man I knew. He was great at talking about his accomplishments, a brilliant golfer, and friends with a lot of the (male) senior managers. But he was also someone who had been more junior than me, so I knew that he wasn't that good. As I sat in my car in the parking lot after hearing this news, in tears of rage and utter frustration, I realised things were different for women. I pledged there and then to make changes. To succeed I needed to wake up and learn from the men around me, from the few senior women who had made it to the top, and from the research available how to claim my rightful place in the corporate world.

And I did. I stepped into my power and made the changes that I'm going to outline to you in the following pages. I was offered a role running a global respiratory health business, which included the launch of an allergy medicine that was the company's biggest ever consumer launch. I have now lived and worked in six countries: Canada, the UK, Cyprus, Dubai, Malaysia and the US. I achieved all this with a family that moved with me – and I learned a lot on the journey.

I now teach and coach women on my unwritten rules of women's leadership. My curriculum covers all the aspects of a corporate career that women often struggle with, and the obstacles they may meet or unwittingly put in their own way.

All career journeys have accelerators and decelerators – toxic cultures, discrimination and unconscious bias are all real and require systemic change. I believe that change will come from outside pressure (equal pay reporting is a good example of this) as well as from within. The best way to get more women into senior leadership is to get more women into senior leadership. This book isn't about 'fixing women' – women don't need to be fixed. My work focuses on how we can maximise the accelerators in our career and navigate the decelerators and obstacles, and ultimately succeed. We all have opportunities to lift others as we rise and to create sisterhood and support for others behind us.

It's vitally important to have women in leadership roles, not only to promote the principles of diversity and equality, but in order for individual women to be able to fulfil their potential. It's a fact that businesses with women on the board and in senior roles perform better than businesses that don't. New research shows that, over the past two decades, in the two years after a new CEO appointment, the stock price for those companies that appointed female CEOs outperformed those that appointed men by an average of 20%.

2020 has been a year of unprecedented change and hardship for many, and yet those of us 'knowledge workers' who can work remotely have been fortunate to still be able to work. As we both move through the public health challenges into the economic trials ahead, I see advantages and disadvantages for women. The shift to greater flexibility around remote working and the decrease in travel are long overdue and will benefit us all. However, the closure of schools and daycare centres has highlighted how important childcare is in the ability of single parents and dual career couples to work and I see that their closure has placed a huge additional burden on all of us, but especially women. We know that the data shows that women are disproportionately affected in economic downturn and periods of job loss, and the issues that women often face in making their work visible and finding the mentors and sponsors that they need could be even worse in an era of remote working. The tools in this book and the sisterhood that we can build together are even more important now to help you navigate your version of success – whether you work in an office or remotely.

This book is based on my journey and my experience as a British, cis, middle-class, able-bodied white woman and, despite the ups and downs of my corporate journey, I know that I have had income and privilege that many others have not. Women of colour, LGBTQ women and those with disabilities face all the issues I faced as well as additional microaggressions, discrimination and unconscious bias barriers too. These women face more barriers to advancement and get less support than other groups of women, face far more everyday discrimination such as having their judgement questioned, being interrupted, or having their ideas co-opted. They are also far more likely than other women to hear demeaning remarks about themselves or others like them.

The world of work doesn't just need the voices of women, it needs the voices of *all* women. I haven't walked their journeys so I don't pretend to speak to those challenges, but I am committed to listening and learning and using my role to drive change for us all. On my podcast and in my community I invite a diverse group of women to share their learnings and resources so that we can all hear and learn from their lessons. When women succeed, we all succeed.

This book is a detailed exploration of all you need to know and do to navigate and thrive. Now is the time to learn from my unwritten rules and find your own, to gain acknowledgement for your achievements, set your sights on where you want to go and claim the leadership that is rightfully yours.

ONE

My Corporate Career Journey

I grew up as the daughter of an accountant who worked for a big company. In my father's eyes, being a director in a big company was the path to success, so I majored in business. As I explored different areas of study, marketing drew me in. Understanding consumer behaviour and why people buy things sounded fascinating.

My third year at college gave me the opportunity to intern with a corporation. I spent a year working in marketing at the corporate offices of the supermarket chain ASDA, which is now owned by Walmart®. At the end of the year, I realised I wanted to work in an environment where I could learn even more about marketing. As I approached graduation, I applied to global companies like Unilever, Mars and Procter & Gamble. They're virtually universities of corporate marketing.

I was excited to join a major corporation and spent two years in a management development programme, which taught me a tremendous amount about marketing. The early days of my career went well. When you're in your twenties, you don't notice the corporate gender gap. The management training programme rotated us around different departments. No one gets promoted at that stage, so it was hard work but fairly straightforward.

I didn't see men moving ahead of me, though I did note almost all senior management positions were filled by men. I noticed it was easier for the men to be friends with senior men than it was for the women. The guys would play golf together, go for a beer and compare football teams. They also seemed to travel together more often.

After five years, the company began to globalise. This led to a change in my role, which removed some of the strategic thinking I enjoyed. I looked for a job where I could continue to grow my marketing career and moved to a major pharmaceutical company.

As I progressed, corporate life began to grow more complex to navigate as a woman. The sales team's nickname for me was 'Legs'. There were few senior female leaders who could be a role model for me.

Perceptions

In her 2004 *Harvard Business Review* article, psychiatrist
Anna Fels states:

> 'Women have more opportunities for forming
> and pursuing their own goals now than at
> any time in history. But doing so is socially
> condoned only if they have first satisfied the
> needs of all their family members: husbands,
> children, elderly parents and others.'

It seems paradoxical to me. We have hard-won access
to training in nearly all fields, but far from celebrating
our achievements in the professions now available to
us, most of us deflect attention away from ourselves.
We often don't claim a central, purposeful place in our
own stories. We eagerly shift credit elsewhere and shun
recognition. And it's not only women of achievement
who are anxious to relinquish recognition – it's nearly
all women. Studies show that the daily texture of wom-
en's lives from childhood onward is one filled with
micro-encounters in which quiet withdrawal and the
transfer of attention or recognition to others is expected,
particularly in the presence of men.

Despite societal expectations to push attention away
from ourselves, as professional women, we must climb
the corporate ladder. If we don't speak up, we'll be left
behind or asked to leave. In most organisations, it's
move up or you're out.

But there are differences in the way women and men are treated as they seek to climb the ladder. When we openly express our ambition, we're perceived as being harsh or strident. For example, I doubt the negative feedback I received for my behaviours in a 360-degree assessment would have been considered negative if the same behaviours had been observed in a man. I was told people viewed me as 'out for myself'.

'What's wrong with caring about progressing in my career?' I thought. 'What do you expect? Everyone wants to move up.' I was frustrated by the double standard. I didn't know what the real issue was, because there was no one to tell me the unwritten rules.

Working for a global company provided opportunities to work overseas. I moved to Cyprus in 1998 and became the third female expatriate in the company. In this massive company that employed 50,000 people, there were only two other women on overseas assignments at the time. I was also their first female employee to give birth abroad. There was some confusion about how to deal with my pregnancy and maternity leave, and no policy for managers working abroad. I felt they were concerned I would quit so I was extremely quick to correct them and let them know I would be coming back (and soon). I gave birth four weeks early.

My maternity leave was only one week long because I wouldn't hand over my job to anyone. Back then, that was fine by me. I ran the consumer business, and we were busy. For five weeks, I worked from home (they wouldn't let me set foot in the office because of the insurance). I simply asked the people I was due to have meetings with to come to my apartment, and I kept up with all my emails. I didn't stop working because I didn't want to step off the promotion ladder and harm my career.

If anyone had said to me, 'You should take six months off. You'll want to be with the baby. They grow up so fast, you'll miss it,' I probably wouldn't have listened. Would I recommend my path as the right way for other women? No, but it was right for me then. You should do whatever feels right for you.

The dangers of the 'mummy track' are real though. Ariane Hegewisch, Program Director for employment earnings at the Institute for Women's Policy Research in Washington, said, 'Evidence from a variety of countries reveals that the longer new mothers are away from paid work, the less likely they are to be promoted, move into management, or receive a pay raise once their leave is over. They are also at greater risk of being fired or demoted.' A 2014 survey of more than 25,000 Harvard Business School graduates found women in fields like finance and consulting reported that taking more than six months of leave hurt them professionally.

Admittedly, the path I took would be considered extreme today. My advice is to choose what works best for you. If you want time with your new baby, do it. If you want to return right away, do it. No one else can tell you what's right for you.

I also noticed I was treated differently once my first child was born. My boss was genuinely concerned and asked how I was doing all the time. 'How are you?' he'd ask. 'Did you sleep? Is Alex OK? Is everything all right?'

I finally told him to stop asking. 'Look,' I said. 'Can we make an agreement that you simply don't ask? If everything's not fine, I'll certainly tell you.' He was trying to be supportive, but I didn't want to be treated differently from men whose wives had had a baby.

Taking a chance on a woman

Later in my career, I was placed in a programme for high-potential leaders.

'Why are you still a Marketing Director?' a senior leader asked me. 'Why aren't you a Vice President yet?'

'I don't know, Stan. I don't know why I can't seem to break through,' I answered.

'It seems to me,' he said, 'nobody is prepared to take a chance on you.'

And he was right. No one was prepared to see the potential of what I could do and take a chance on me.

I was viewed as 'risky', even though I had an amazing track record of achievements globally. Despite my successes, I couldn't shatter the glass ceiling.

After a while, a new position in his group came up. The role was somewhat vague and undefined. He walked into my office, closed the door and took a seat.

'I've got a role spearheading a new team,' he said. 'It's not working on an existing brand. It's exploring what our future global brands will be. Are you brave?'

Someone was finally willing to take a chance on me and see my potential. I said 'yes' immediately.

The new job pulled me into a higher peer group and got me onto the leadership team with the Vice Presidents. I participated in top-level meetings and became more visible. I proved I could do it and was later promoted to Vice President too. I'll always be grateful to Stan because he saw I could lead a business and operate at a senior level.

A 2011 McKinsey study discussed the contrast in how men and women are judged for promotion. Women are more likely to be promoted based on their track record while men are more likely to be promoted based on their potential. For example, let's assume a man and woman have completed A, B and C in their careers. They both apply for a promotion which will require them to do D, necessary for the next level up.

In reviewing applicants, employers evaluate the man and say, 'He's done A, B and C. He's got such potential. Therefore, he can certainly do D!'

When they evaluate the woman, who's also accomplished A, B and C, they say, 'She's only done A, B and C. She's never performed D before. She's not qualified for this role.' That's unconscious bias. And this reflects what Stan said when he noted, 'No one's taken a chance on you.'

During the four years I was a fully-fledged Vice President, a realisation grew within me. While I liked and even loved what I did, I finally realised, 'I'm doing this because it's what my dad wanted. It doesn't feed my soul and never did. What feeds my soul is growing people, how can I do more of it?'

At the time, I was working with an executive coach.

'I get to travel business class,' I told him. 'I get limos to pick me up from my house and take me to the airport. I get to say I'm a Vice President.'

'All that stuff,' my coach said, 'keeps you comfortable. It's all good, but it can get in the way of *great*.' He was right.

Jim Collins, in his ground-breaking 2001 book, *Good to Great*, said:

'When what you are deeply passionate
about – what you can be best in the world
at – and what drives your economic engine
come together, not only does your work move
toward greatness, but so does your life. For,
in the end, it's impossible to have a great life
unless it's a meaningful life.'

I developed and started implementing a five-year plan
to become an executive coach and corporate trainer. As
part of my plan, before leaving, I wanted to complete
our work on a major project. I wanted to leave on a
high note.

A year before the launch, my boss and I were talking
about what I should do next. I'd been in the role of Vice
President for two and a half years.

'Leave me on the project, but once it's launched, I intend
to leave the company,' I told him.

He was surprised, and he wasn't pleased, but that's
what happened. Even though he offered alternatives,
they simply left me cold. I knew I wouldn't want to get
out of bed in the morning if I was doing those other
projects. No longer would I allow good to get in the
way of my great.

After the launch, I started the next chapter of my career
and my business. In June 2015, I left corporate life and
Powerful Growth Group was born.

Looking back with pride

I'm grateful for all the opportunities that working for major companies gave me and there are many things that I'm proud of in my career. One particular highlight was achieving the switch of the leading allergy medicine from prescription to over-the-counter status. The company had tried to get this project off the ground a decade earlier, but it had become stuck in internal issues. I led the team and we broke the deadlock. My team and our agencies developed all the materials, the advertising, the packaging and the launch advertising. The product quickly grew into a huge business with half a billion dollars annually in global sales.

So much of what I enjoyed at work was developing and growing the people in my teams and I'm proud that many of these people and others I mentored or coached over the years have continued to succeed in senior roles all over the world. As leaders, our real legacy is the people we grow and help to succeed.

And counting the mistakes…

But, when I reflect on my career and how I stumbled before learning the unwritten rules, I realise I made the same mistakes millions of women make in business.

If I could go back and coach myself when I was younger, these are the pitfalls I would warn myself about:

- I did a poor job with stakeholder management

- I did a horrible job of making my work visible and I undersold my strengths

- I took conflict far too personally

- And, as a working mum, I held a lot of guilt because I felt I left work too early and got home too late

If I had known then what I know now, I'd have managed myself differently. I would talk more about what I did and the value I added. I would find mentors and sponsors and manage stakeholders differently. I'd learn to manage conflict with ease and, finally, I'd stop feeling guilty about my kids or my career.

Later in my career, once I had understood the unwritten rules, I left my doubts and reticence behind and eventually excelled. I finally broke through, but it could have been easier, which is why I have written the book that I needed to read back then, for you now.

TWO

It All Starts With Self-leadership

Before you can lead other people or an organisation, you must effectively lead yourself. Ultimately, you're the only person you can control at work and throughout your life. Let's focus first on how you become a pro at self-leadership.

Change always starts with you. If you're unaware of these basics and of the unwritten rules of self-leadership, it'll slow down your path to success. Self-leadership skills are the most basic foundations for your journey toward greater success.

You can control your emotions

Women on the corporate path often have tremendous ambition to succeed and move up, but along the way there will be moments when the sense of injustice and disappointment becomes overwhelming. Believe me, I cried silently in the bathroom many times until I learned this rule.

The solution is to exploit the momentary gap of time between your thoughts, your emotions and your reaction to every situation. It may whizz by you as you react spontaneously, but you can control in an instant how you respond to every circumstance. You need to look for that precise moment and ask, 'Where's my mood at right now?'

If you're in a funk or feeling angry with a co-worker, do you think this is the best way to step into your next encounter with your boss? When you're challenged in a meeting, or if someone speaks to you rudely, is your annoyance the best place from which to respond? Probably not.

Leading yourself means choosing to control how you handle stimuli, emotions and events as they come into your brain and how you react or respond. We can't control other people, their reactions or what they say, so the best place to start as a leader is by mastering how you lead yourself.

The thirteenth-century scholar, poet and mystic Rumi said, 'Yesterday I was clever, so I wanted to change the world. Today I am wise, so I am changing myself.'

Start by understanding and watching where you're at on the Mood Elevator.

Adopt a mood of curiosity

The Mood Elevator is a model developed by Larry Senn of Senn Delaney in the 1970s. It was designed to help you determine where your mood and emotions are. The higher you rise on the elevator, the more positive your emotions. As you go down on the elevator, the more negative your emotions become – feelings such as impatience, frustration and irritation appear on the ladder. Beneath that are worry, anxiety, defensiveness, insecurity, judgement, blame, self-righteousness, stress, burnout, anger, depression, apathy and shame. Nothing good happens at the bottom of the Mood Elevator. No innovations, problem-solving, agreements or creativity spring from there.

In the middle of the elevator floors are the emotions of curiosity and interest.

How do you manage your mood? Let's say a presentation didn't go well. Your mood drops. But you don't have to climb up from depressed and frustrated to over-the-moon enthusiastic and ebullient. It's difficult to move from the bottom to the top floors. What you can do is switch from anger or disappointment to curiosity.

Shifting from being frustrated or disappointed, for example, to curious and interested, being open to learn, is a big, positive step. You can address questions and solve problems from a more open, receptive place.

Working from curious and interested and moving up the Mood Elevator, what moods or emotions will you notice? Flexibility, adaptability, humour, patience, understanding, appreciation, hopefulness, optimism, resourcefulness, creativity, innovation, wisdom and insight are all there.

At the top floor of the Mood Elevator is gratitude. If a client moans about their job or boss, I'll say, 'Let's shift your mood. Tell me three things you're grateful about in this job.' They might reply with, 'I'm grateful the commute is short. I'm grateful it gets me wonderful exposure. And I'm grateful that on most days my boss is nice.' (This is a useful technique whatever your situation: write down three things you're grateful for every morning and watch your mood lift.)

Become a good observer of your emotions and reactions so you can move up on the elevator.

Getting onto the balcony in our lives

As you move up, the next step is changing your perception of a situation. Most people live 100% 'in the dance'. Imagine you're in an elegant ballroom and the evening's dance is the waltz. You have some experience, but there are steps you haven't yet mastered. A lot is happening as you move around the dancefloor.

You think, 'One-two-three, where do my feet go? Where do my arms go? What's Prince Charming doing on the other side of the ballroom with Cinderella? One-two-three. Right, left, right, left.' You're completely in the moment and you are reacting to what's taking place around you.

But to operate effectively, you need to be able to be mentally in two places at once. If you can shift your mental focus, so that you can not only be in the dance but watching yourself from the balcony too, you'll become a better observer of where you're at and the stimuli around you.

I suggest you keep only 70% of yourself in the dance, with 30% of your awareness focused on watching and observing. This is how you will discover more about yourself and your emotions.

Try it and see what you learn about yourself by watching from the balcony. By keeping 30% of your focus on being an observer, you will have the presence of mind to choose your floor on the Mood Elevator and make better decisions in the moment.

Your perception is your reality

When it comes to work, there's rarely absolute truth. For example, if you work in marketing and you believe sales are down 20% because the sales team is not performing, you're likely to be strongly attached to this point of view. If you work in sales, you might believe sales are down 20% because the marketing materials are wrong and aren't helping the sales team.

Are they right, or am I right? What is the truth? We will never definitively know – they're simply each side's point of view. Your perception is your reality. The other person's perception is their reality. Our internal filters shape our perceptions and how we see the world. Those filters come from how you were raised, where you've been and what you've experienced.

Everyone thinks they see life as it really is, as if they're looking through a clear lens, with no distortion. However, your view isn't the same as everyone else's because of your internal filters. These filters are such an intrinsic part of you that you may not be aware of them. If you always wear glasses with red lenses, everything looks red. If you wear glasses with blue lenses, everything looks blue. As life happens and you have more experiences, you add more filters.

Think back to when you were an infant and you didn't have any filters. As you grew into childhood, perhaps you were told 'no' over and over. Or you heard, 'Don't do that!' and, 'You're such an idiot!' Over time you would have added filters. Say you were bullied at school: that would have added another filter. You were dumped by your boyfriend. You rose to the top of the class. Or you weren't picked for the sports team. Each experience would have shaped your perception and the way you viewed yourself and your life.

This would have all happened at a subconscious level. You didn't realise those experiences had created your filters. By the time you're in your thirties, you're wearing multiple pairs of glasses and are completely unaware of how they obscure your vision.

Of course, my glasses are different from yours. When we sit down to talk about sales and marketing, I'll perceive the world differently from you. But if you were wearing the exact same glasses, we'd see the world the same way.

Shift your mindset to the belief that there is no one 'truth'. There's your point of view and their point of view. Now, move up on the Mood Elevator to curious and interested. Then you can open a conversation like this:

'I'm curious, Jim. Tell me why you think you need more help in marketing. What seems to not be working? Tell me why you think that is? How can I help?'

Suddenly the conversation becomes less personal. You're no longer your own reaction. This distinction can help you manage how you present yourself and build relationships instead of jockeying for control. Compare an angry response with: 'That's interesting. We have two different points of view, so let's try to understand each other.' One conversation will help get you promoted and the other will keep you stuck.

Are you a victim or an owner?

A person with an 'owner' mindset fundamentally believes they can control their lives. They take responsibility for their lives. They own their circumstances, so life happens *for* them, instead of to them. People who create a habit of thinking as an owner usually embrace change. They:

- Have a growth mindset

- Hold an optimistic outlook on life

- Look for opportunities to create

- See problems as puzzles to be solved

- Take full responsibility for their happiness

- Look at challenges as opportunities

Contrast this with a victim mindset. How do victims recognise or define themselves? They:

- Have a learned way of behaving as a victim

- Come from a place of 'Oh, poor me!'

- Feel that things just happen to them

- Don't embrace or even like change

- Live with a fixed mindset rather than a growth mindset

What is a fixed mindset? In *Mindset: The new psychology of success*, Stanford University psychologist Carol Dweck says:

> 'People with a fixed mindset believe their basic qualities, like their intelligence or talent, are simply fixed traits. They spend their time documenting their intelligence or talent instead of developing them.'

A person with a fixed mindset says, 'I'm not the kind of person who does...' Or, 'I don't do...' Or, 'I'm not the kind of person who apologises.'

Yet a fixed position is often easily abandoned. If you were to say to them, 'If I give you a million dollars, would you apologise?' most of the time they would say 'yes'. They are the kind of person who can apologise. They simply choose not to.

Dweck also says:

> 'In a growth mindset, people believe their most basic abilities can be developed through dedication and hard work – brains and talent are just the starting point. This view creates a love of learning and a resilience essential for accomplishment.'

In contrast, victims rarely take responsibility. Their behaviour becomes most obvious when things go wrong. Victims say things like:

- 'Sales didn't provide us with the right material.'

- 'The deadlines are simply unreasonable.'

- 'The traffic was horrible this morning.'

Remember when we discuss 'victim mindset' here we are discussing a mindset and not the state of being a victim in its usual sense and use of the word. This distinction doesn't negate the fact that bad things happen to people that aren't their fault at all. We are using the 'victim' word to describe a mindset here.

For victims, life is happening to them all the time. Victims are pessimistic, they complain, blame others for their circumstances, are defined by their past, have a 'poor me' attitude, and constantly expect sympathy. Being a victim in life is easier, but it's less effective and it almost always results in going backwards rather than forwards.

Contrast this with an owner who says, 'I'm sorry I'm late, I didn't leave enough time for the morning traffic.' Imagine yourself making each of those statements and the emotions that would accompany them. It's about taking responsibility for your life and your choices.

As with everything to do with your emotions and mindset, you get to choose between being a victim or an owner. Victims and owners can be in extremely different places on the Mood Elevator.

You're continuously creating your world. People with an owner mindset say:

- 'I get to pick up my kids from school.'

- 'I choose to go to work this morning.'

- 'I want to work on my relationship with my spouse.'

- 'I commit to doing an excellent job on this project.'

- 'I will create a win–win solution.'

You can be an owner most of the time, but there are moments when you might need to vent or whine for five minutes. Everyone's entitled to the odd 'whiny-victim' moment.

When I give myself five minutes to be a victim, that 30% of myself on the balcony hears the moaning. After a couple of minutes, I'm laughing at the absurdity of it all. After five minutes, I've had enough, because it didn't change anything. The good news is, I'm then ready to move forwards to feeling curious and to ask, 'What will I do about it?' It's time to get creative, resourceful and innovative.

Everything starts with yourself as you grow in leadership. Self-leadership is not about what you face in your career and life, but about how you handle it.

THREE

Standing In Your Power

Think of a leader you admire. People who are well-regarded and seen as leaders usually exude confidence and they hold their ground in discussions. When we watch them in a meeting, we feel 100% certain they must know what they're saying. They have an 'I can handle it' air as they move with unruffled ease through whatever comes their way.

Increasing your confidence will change the way you are perceived by your co-workers, your team and even your boss – you will gain authority and earn greater respect. But how do you move past the fear of the unknown? How do you quell the monkey chatter in your mind shouting, 'Who do you think you are?'

In this chapter, I'll provide simple strategies to help you not only appear more confident, but also to start feeling more confident inside. It's not difficult, but it requires steady application before it feels natural and an authentic part of you.

Understand the difference between confidence and courage

Most people think you must possess confidence before doing something new and scary. I don't see confidence as a prerequisite: it's an output. You gain confidence after doing something new. You feel more confident about the possibility of doing it again and of doing other new things.

Courage is essential before doing something new and scary. My definition of courage is 'feeling the fear and doing it anyway'. If you're not getting outside your comfort zone and growing, you're not trying hard enough. Growth and expansion don't happen in your comfort zone. When you feel scared, it's a sign you're on your leadership edge. As you grow, it's amazing how much easier things become.

Jumping in on a webinar with twenty women or leading a workshop used to feel edgy to me. Courage got me through it the first few times, but now I'm comfortable. In fact, I love it, because I've done it over and over until I became competent and confident at it.

Appear confident on the outside

When you lack confidence in certain moments, how can you appear more confident on the outside? How do you let others perceive you as present, well-prepared and confident? You can demonstrate outer confidence through:

- Your body language or posture

- Using good eye contact

- Your spoken and written words

- Your tone of voice

What energy do you bring to the room with your body language? Are you excited? Fidgety? Does your body language make you appear nervous? Or is it purposeful and in control? Chapter 6 contains detailed information on posture and positioning. For now, I want to focus on confident behaviours.

If you're speaking in a meeting, introduce yourself and shake hands with as many people as you can. In a business setting, you normally know everyone. If there's anyone you don't know, demonstrate confidence by shaking hands firmly and introducing yourself. If you're speaking onstage, get comfortable with the space beforehand. Go there at the beginning of the meeting as people file in. Stand where you'll speak and look at where the audience will be seated. Get comfortable and own the space. Take a few deep breaths and open your body language.

Strong eye contact gives you the appearance of confidence. If you struggle with eye contact, have a strategy for it while you're in a meeting. Choose who you'll look at. One good eye contact strategy is to connect with the person in charge and then others. Make sure you're not looking down at your documents or off into the distance. Averting your gaze will make you appear less confident.

A friend told me she found eye contact uncomfortable. Her eye contact strategy is to look at the other person's nose. They think she's making eye contact and she is often complimented for having great eye contact. Other people focus on one eye at a time, especially while up close.

Lowering the pitch and speed of your voice will bring a calm, positive energy to your words. Match the energy of the room and be purposeful about how you use your voice.

Avoid using leaky language

Women often give away their power with what I call 'leaky language'. They can lose power and confidence with the words they speak or write. They apologise too much and say weak things like:

- 'Sorry to suggest this, but...'

- 'It may not be a good idea, but...'

- 'I just want to say...'

Anything you say or write with words like 'just', 'sorry' or with an apologetic tone gives away your power, your confidence and makes you appear less authoritative. At times, we say words like this to fill an uncomfortable silence and make the request seem more pleasant. Resist the temptation to do this. Ask for what you want or make your point and don't add apologies or anything that diminish who you are and what you have to add. A few moments of silence are far better than speaking leaky words and phrases which drain you of your power.

I frequently encounter women among my clients and on courses who admit they do this. In fact, I've had women tell me minutes after our meeting or training has concluded that they've caught themselves writing 'just' in an email and deleted it.

Saying 'sorry' is the most serious use of leaky language by women. Women seem to say the word 'sorry' far more than men. If you truly have done something wrong, then apologise. If you back into someone and spill coffee on them, of course you should say 'sorry'. If you miss a deadline or don't deliver something that's expected of you, say 'I'm sorry' and then say what you intend to do to fix the problem.

But don't say 'I'm sorry' as a way of entering a conversation or sharing your point of view. If you say it when there's nothing to apologise for, it diminishes you as a person who has valuable insight to add and it takes away from your status as a leader. Instead, choose language that projects confidence and self-assurance. Say:

- 'I have another perspective I'd like to share...'

- 'After reviewing the deck, I notice...'

- 'It's possible we may be missing something. I suggest...'

Phrases like these keep you in your power and position you as a leader. It signals that what you have to share has merit. It also says, 'I'm in this meeting because I deserve to be here and my contributions have value for what we're working to accomplish.'

Manage impostor syndrome

Impostor syndrome is when a person feels they're not good enough. Feeling inadequate and fearing that your secret inadequacy might be discovered is at the heart of impostor syndrome. Many people experience these feelings, not just women. Almost every male CEO I've coached has suffered from it.

A few days after I was promoted to Vice President, I was sitting in a regular meeting. Everybody was talking and making suggestions. Then I spoke, and I noticed everyone write down what I had to say. I watched them all dutifully jot down notes and I thought, 'Whoa! What just happened?' When I had spoken a few days before my promotion, no one wrote it down. My impostor syndrome was triggered. I thought, 'I don't know any more than I did last week. This is crazy! I don't deserve that. I don't have all the answers.'

In a 2006 study conducted by Shamala Kumar and Carolyn Jagacinski involving 135 college students, women who attained high scores indicating impostor syndrome found that they worked and competed harder to prove themselves. Conversely, men feeling similarly uncertain avoided situations where their weaknesses could be exposed. Their motivation was to constantly look strong by engaging in activities likely to showcase their strengths.

Impostor thoughts will send you straight down in the Mood Elevator. To manage impostor syndrome when it pops up then, you must bring your emotions back up to 'curious'.

A talented friend of mine recently started a new job. She's dealing with her own version of impostor syndrome every day. Meeting people who have worked for amazing, prestigious companies, she feels both unprepared and inadequate.

I pointed out to her, 'When you feel like an impostor, or as if you're not good enough, you're being selfish. Stop it. When you feel like an impostor, you're focused on you and whether you're good enough. You're in your head, thinking about you.'

In this situation, you need to redirect your energy and your focus on them, the people at your company and your customers. They've already decided you're good enough because they hired you. Return to a place of 'curious' on the Mood Elevator and think of yourself as a learner. Ask:

- What am I here to do for these people?
- What do they need?
- How can I help them?

If you try to show up as an expert, it's easier to feel like an impostor. Focus on being of service, rather than on being an expert. I don't love the notion of 'fake it till you make it'. Consider 'practising the future' instead. It looks like this: if I were an expert or a person with a more senior role, what would I be? How would I show up? Try it on and step into that role.

Fully owning your strengths and talents is an antidote to impostor syndrome. Remind yourself where you're strong, what you're good at, how you make a difference and how far you've come. Expressing your strengths through the scope of your expertise makes you more powerful than if you act as if you know everything. You might say, 'Here's where I can really help.' Or, 'These are the three areas where I can really help. Let's bring the rest of the team in on these other areas, which will pull in their expertise and resources.'

Make friends with your inner critic

We all have an inner critic. If a voice in your head just said, 'I don't have one', then you just heard it! The inner critic is the voice in your head commenting on you, your life and surroundings. It says negative things like:

- You're not good enough.

- You failed before, you'll probably fail again.

- Who are you to think you can do this?

It's not actually you, it's your ego talking. Our egos can often be critical, cruel and say things you'd never say to your worst enemy. The inner critic also says things that are untrue. These voices are from your past, trying to keep you small, safe and protected. Their purpose is to 'help' you survive. If you're just puttering quietly at home, the voices are quiet. When you do brave, edgy things, that's when they shout.

Write down what your inner critic says. It's important that you see it on paper. When you do, you'll realise how cruel it is. Where does that voice come from in your past? Is there a person you recognise, or an event you remember those cruel words from? The person may not have even said those words, but they led to you feel and think those thoughts.

Give your inner critic a name. I named my inner critic 'Hamster', because it keeps me running on a hamster wheel of achievement. Then, have a conversation with it and use its name. Since your inner critic (the ego) is trying to protect you, tell it you no longer need its protection. Say something like: 'Thank you, Hamster. I'm OK, I know you're trying to protect me. I know you believe you have my best interest at heart, but I'm growing. You can relax now. I can handle this.'

Many people believe in fighting their inner critic. That's a mistake because the more you fight, the harder it will fight back. Those voices will never entirely go away. However, you can quiet them by replacing your inner critic with your inner coach. Your inner coach is the voice you needed to hear when you were young. It's the one that encourages you and buoys you up. Move your thoughts to what you most wanted to hear when you were young. The sentence you choose will be meaningful to you. What did you most want to hear when you were growing up? Mine is: 'You're enough without your achievements.' That's what I wish I was told growing up, and that's what I tell my inner critic now.

The voices can be loud at times and they don't stop, even when you continue to choose growth. The tasks or work you've mastered may no longer trigger your inner critic, but when you venture into something new, the voices may resume their chatter.

Get comfortable with the reality of failure

I used to have an unhealthy relationship with failure. That's true of many highly driven people. But now I accept the fact it happens at times, so a more helpful way to view failure is as a valuable learning experience.

'I don't mind losing as long as I see improvement, or feel I've done as well as I possibly could. Failure is information,' says Carol Dweck, author of *Mindset: The New Psychology of Success*.

Over time, I've grown conscious of the feelings that arise when I reach the edge of my comfort zone. Those feelings can be uncomfortable and unsettling. Then I remember, I'm right where I'm supposed to be. I'm growing.

Keep a Success File

I keep a file filled with letters, printouts of emails, cards of thanks and notes about the difference I've made, how I've impacted lives and my achievements. You could keep one on your computer instead. When I have a rough moment that is hard to reframe as a 'learning experience' because it still feels raw, I'll read through those cards and emails to remind myself how much I've already succeeded and made a difference. They always manage to remind me that I am doing well and making a positive impact on the people I help.

Develop your own Success File as a concrete way to remind yourself that you are making a difference. Over time you'll fill it with thank yous and acknowledgements that you find encouraging. When you have a moment where you need to bring yourself up, you'll be able to pull it out to re-read the positive words others have said about you.

Stay in the present

Living in the now is about seeing a clean slate and taking action. I say to my coaching clients, if you want to feel stressed, invent a scary story of what might happen in the future and immerse yourself in thinking about it now. Before you know it, you'll be dropping down in the Mood Elevator all the way to anxiety:

- What if the economy crashes?

- What if nobody needs my skills anymore?

- What if I'm penniless, destitute and on the streets?

Focus on those things and it'll do crazy things in your mind. All of those are stories in the future that probably won't happen. Let's deal with the present and what you can do *now*. Don't get stuck in a fictional story about the future.

You may also stress out by focusing on a horrible story from the past, reflecting on it over and over. Remember when you felt like you weren't enough, and you failed? That's not a helpful place to be in your head. You can shift your mindset by asking what you learned. This will bring you back to the present, where you can act.

Release your need to be perfect

Perfection is the enemy of good. Trying to be perfect often leads to procrastination because you are afraid of getting something wrong. The pursuit of excellence is gratifying and healthy. Pursuing perfection is frustrating, neurotic and a terrible waste of time.

Rather than trying to be flawless all the time, consider what absolutely must be perfect and what doesn't require perfection. Give yourself the grace of not being excellent in every facet of life. Does your desk need to always be perfectly tidy? Do your kitchen counters always need to be perfectly clean? Does everything in your life need to be perfect? No, it doesn't. Choose carefully where you'll be perfect and where you can be 'good enough'.

Confidence comes from knowing, owning and accepting yourself as a work in progress. It's also a result of learning you can do new things. In the meantime, outer confidence can help you exude an air of confidence as you learn and grow.

FOUR

Building Your Brand

The strategic decisions you make will impact your career and as a result, your personal brand. At one point I had to ask myself, 'Do I want to be a general manager, or go down the strategic marketing track?' I hadn't yet decided what my value proposition was or clarified my personal brand.

After I had been running a global marketing team for a while, a senior leader sat me down for a talk. He said, 'Here's what I find intriguing. If I evaluate you against your peers as a general manager, you rank OK. You don't have a lot of sales experience or a finance background. But you're an effective leader and you can handle operations well. Competitively, you're probably in the middle.' He stated firmly, 'When I consider the route you could take on the strategic marketing path, you're like no one I've met. No one touches you.' He perceived me as having more competitive edge in marketing compared to general management. This helped me clarify my brand.

My meeting with him was the first time I thought of positioning my career, my brand, in a competitive way. Until this conversation, I had always asked myself questions like, 'Which role would I enjoy more? Which works with my lifestyle?' Looking at my career from a competitive angle was an important breakthrough. Your strategic career choices based on where you can shine is a personal branding decision, too.

After that discussion, I was no longer indecisive. I was clear I wanted to build my skills and experience as a strategic marketer. Making that firm decision changed my brand and career forever. To begin managing your career direction and brand, ask yourself three questions:

- To understand where you are today, ask: 'Where do I stand out and excel naturally?'

- Then: 'Where can I best position myself competitively?'

- Finally, ask: 'How can I focus my attention on becoming known for excellence in my niche?'

Proactively own and manage your personal brand

You probably know you should brand yourself, but you may not understand how to do it.

Let's start by defining what branding is in the context of your career. Branding is everything about the experience of working or doing business with you. It's your image and reputation, built not only on what you do but also your way of being and how you appear in your role. Branding involves every touchpoint people have with you, including their experiences of you both online and offline. If you don't control your brand and reputation, others will.

Consider yourself as the CEO of your own business – you. What should you do to make sure your brand is as crystal clear as it possibly can be?

The answer lies in three simple steps:

1. Understand where your brand is at currently

2. Understand where you want your brand to be

3. Communicate your brand to the organisation and to senior leaders

To start the journey to discover your brand, you may want to consider:

- What am I good at right now?

- How do I approach my work and career?

- What do I want to step into and become?

- What value proposition do others see in me?

That last bullet is important. Sometimes what others see in us we miss ourselves. It takes objectivity and an ability to see where you fit into the bigger picture to craft a branding or image statement.

To gain insight into your workplace image, ask colleagues for their perceptions of you. Choose five people you work with and ask each of them to provide you with six adjectives that capture how they see you. Ask for three positive attributes and three areas for growth.

One person might give you the positive adjectives 'intelligent', 'driven' and 'creative'. The areas for growth might include 'impatient', 'disorganised' and 'lacks presentation skills'. This would give you a starting point for defining your brand.

After talking with five people, you'll have thirty defining words – fifteen notes of positive feedback and fifteen words representing areas for growth. You may notice some overlap or see a few surprises, but this can be helpful for your understanding. Use your colleagues' feedback to assess your current brand further by asking questions like:

- What skills are essential to performing well in my role?

- What do I bring that's personal and unique?

- What brand do others see in me and my work?

- Where do I have room for growth and improvement?

- Am I a leader? Or...

- ...am I ready to step into leadership?

- Do my colleagues and bosses feel at ease interacting with me?

Once you have understood more about your brand by asking yourself and your colleagues the above questions, you'll be able to create a personal branding statement. Using your own words or the ones given to you, experiment until you have a succinct, powerful statement that lets others know who you are, what you do well and where you're heading. A few examples could be:

- I'm a developer of people and high-performing teams

- I'm a leader who turns failing businesses around

- I bring innovation and fresh ideas to business problems

- I untangle complex business projects and problems

Communicate your brand through education

This is the step where you communicate your brand to senior leaders and others within your organisation.

Most women I've met think talking about themselves is bragging and unattractive. It's an area where we face some of our biggest challenges, so we tend to avoid it. In an in-depth survey, 326 senior executive women across North America were asked how they perceived their strengths and weaknesses, level of career satisfaction, and what steps they were taking to break through to the next level. Of the five areas of career success tracked in the study, women gave themselves the lowest scores in self-initiation and self-promotion demonstrating the struggle this is for women in comparison to men. This reluctance to advocate for oneself may come across as a lack of self-confidence and uncertainty.

A 2014 study published by Jessi L Smith, Professor of Psychology at Montana State University, found gender norms help explain why women feel uncomfortable discussing their own accomplishments. Smith asked college-aged women to write two letters of recommendation for a scholarship. One was for a friend, the other was on their own behalf. The letters written for friends were considerably better in quality than the letters written for themselves. Why did they have such a hard time writing on their own behalf? Psychologists say engaging in an activity that violates our 'modesty norm' triggers anxiety and, ultimately, produces poorer out-comes. Fear of 'unladylike' bragging stresses women out.

The good news is, when provided with instruction and encouragement, women can communicate more effectively about their successes. The way that feels more authentic to me is to see talking about myself as 'education' rather than boasting. When I reframed self-promotion as simply informing others, it was a huge breakthrough. You can help people learn about what you do and achieve rather than keeping it a secret.

You know who you are and where you're at in your career. You've decided what your value proposition is, based on what you bring and how you're different. You know you're exceptionally good at what you do. Blending this with being adept at how you talk about your achievements is a powerful combination. It took me years to discover how to express what I was good at and to do it with finesse.

For years, I didn't realise meeting with senior leaders to discuss my career and achievements was even an option. I didn't know my male colleagues put time in senior leaders' calendars to talk about themselves. They were more proactive than women when asking for time with senior managers, and took the initiative to promote themselves. By doing this, they got personal time to:

- Make themselves and their work visible
- Talk about their careers
- Share their aspirations
- Ask for new assignments
- Ask for a promotion or a new role

It was almost like a secret club. It made me nauseous when I realised I needed to do it too, because it seemed so incredibly self-serving. I had to force myself, as it felt like shameless self-promotion.

Ask for advice

Eventually I got comfortable about it by asking for advice. I'd book time with a senior leader to ask a specific question about business or my career. People like being asked for advice.

Asking for advice provided me with a platform to learn from and connect with them. I'd talk about what I was doing, what I was delivering and the difference I was making. Sharing this way helped me build my brand and reputation authentically. Coffee with a senior executive with a question to ask for their input was an easy way into a conversation.

When I still lived in Great Britain, I was interested in taking an international assignment abroad and I had a meeting in Australia. I didn't know the Marketing

Director, Clive, but I knew someone who worked on his team. I asked my contact if he'd ask Clive for a meeting on my behalf so I could seek his advice about moving into an international assignment. He agreed, and we met for coffee.

I wanted to work in Australia, but I didn't want to say, 'Can you give me a job?' It felt awkward. Instead I asked his advice about working internationally. He gave me some helpful insight. Then he asked about me and what I'd done.

I was able to talk to him about my journey, my successes, what I had delivered, and my value proposition. He remembered me, and I stayed on his radar. Five years after that conversation over coffee, a role in Dubai as a Marketing Director for the Middle East came up. My name was mentioned, and I learned Clive recommended me.

I got a call and was asked, 'Do you want to work in the Middle East? Clive wants you to be his Marketing Director.' If I hadn't asked Clive for advice several years earlier, I wouldn't have been able to make a positive impression, he would have never known me, and I would never have landed that job.

Be great at what you do

Doing excellent work is the most fundamental thing you can do for your brand. Excellent work is your foundation and strength. If that's missing, nothing else will work. If you're not good at what you do yet, strive to learn and improve so you can deliver on your promises. Acquire the skills you're currently missing so you can perform at peak levels. When you're talented at what you do, you:

- Are resourceful

- Take care of things

- Delegate where you can

- Never blame others

Delivering on your promises means you do what you say you'll do. Instead of resigning yourself to people who don't deliver, learn to delegate so people hit their deadlines. Successful delegating means handing tasks to people on your team and occasionally to some who aren't. If you must, escalate a request to make sure people give you what you need so you can deliver on time. Remember – we only get judged on our visible work.

One branding fiction I hope you never fall prey to, however, is the idea that doing excellent work means you'll magically build an impressive personal brand. Doing your work well and building your brand are not the same activity.

FIVE

Getting Visible

Research shows that the two biggest drivers of success for women are visibility and having mentors and sponsors. So, I want you to read these chapters really carefully! If the thought of promoting yourself at work makes you uncomfortable, you're not alone. Many women feel that way and it holds them back from the success they've worked so hard to attain. Is it holding you back, too? Let's look at some ways to make it easy that will make an enormous difference to how you're perceived and your potential for growth and promotions.

We only get judged on our visible work

There is visible work and invisible work. Think for a moment about the work you do, the value you add and the results you have delivered at work. How much of that is visible to your boss and to those who will make the decision on your next promotion? When I ask that question to a group of women at an event there is usually a collective sigh and comments like 'they don't know the half of what I do' or 'if I left they would need two people to replace me'. Doing your work well and getting credit for it are not the same. Women often put far too much time and attention into invisible work, hoping it'll be noticed and appreciated. It's unrealistic to expect other people to notice you and enquire about what you're doing. It's incumbent on you to reach out and let others know how you add value to your team, your department and your organisation. If you do good work and no one notices, you don't get the credit. Your boss has little idea what you do; they don't understand the effort it might take for you to get from point A to point B, so you are 100% responsible for making your work visible.

Be aware also that you cannot rely on your boss to make your work visible to others; don't think that your boss will telegraph your contributions, skills and strengths. Most bosses are too busy thinking about what they are doing and their own projects. Even if they do promote your achievements, you need to give them talking points in alignment with your brand, so that they do it accurately.

I used to think of this as 'self-promotion', which felt inauthentic and 'yucky' to have to do. When I instead thought about it as educating others on my invisible work, it was a more comfortable way of reframing what was needed. Shifting my perspective was incredibly important in my progression here.

When I became aware of this, I thought, 'Wow, I didn't know people actually did that. Why don't they teach this in business school?' I wish someone had told me sooner. Much of the work I did was good, but it was invisible. As a speaker, trainer and coach, I've learned I'm not the only woman who had no idea I needed to promote myself.

In his book *Empowering Yourself: The organizational game revealed*, author Harvey Coleman says we are evaluated 10% on performance, 30% on impact (appearance) and 60% on exposure and self-promotion.

When I speak to corporate groups, this is one of the crucial unwritten rules I often talk about and it bears repeating. In fact, many of the questions I receive from professional women are around the topic of self-promotion and how to get past the mountain of discomfort associated with it. I understand completely. When you first step past the boundaries of your comfort zone, yes, you will feel uncomfortable. But once you've done it several times, your confidence muscles will grow.

A 2017 study conducted by LinkedIn, the professional social media site, analysed more than 141 *million* member profiles in the United States. They noted that most women have shorter profile summaries describing their accomplishments. Men 'skew their professional brands to highlight more senior-level experience', sometimes even removing their junior roles from their resume. Women shared 11% fewer *skills* on their LinkedIn page compared with their male counterparts. The study also found that women were more likely to apply for administrative roles in marketing and customer service, while men aim for 'higher prestige' and higher paid roles.

A 2011 Catalyst.org study found that women who 'do all the right things' to get ahead still advance less than men and wait longer to receive pay raises. Women who actively attempt to receive high-profile assignments, read career self-help books, ask for help, and build relationships with influential leaders still struggle. However, when women get past their discomfort and self-promote, the results are more promising. According to the study, 'When women were proactive in making their achievements visible, they advanced further... were more satisfied with their careers and had accelerated compensation growth compared to women who were less focused on calling attention to their successes.' You may want to avoid it, but the best way to level the playing field as a woman is self-promotion.

Tara Mohr, a career coach and author of *Playing Big: Practical wisdom for women who want to speak up, create, and lead* says: 'It's tricky for women to talk about our own accomplishments and abilities. We tend to be judged more harshly than men for self-promoting, particularly when other women do the judging.'

I was recently asked to write a reference letter for a former client. I was happy to help, because she was brilliant, and asked her to write a first draft so the letter included all the important things she wanted covered. I asked her to write it as if she was writing about someone else.

She told me later she was initially uncomfortable writing the first draft, because it felt like she was bragging about herself. Framing it as if she was writing about someone else helped her get through it.

This is an area in which you can offer valuable support to other women in the workplace – drafting a document that outlines a colleague's qualities and achievements as you see them could help someone reluctant to articulate their accomplishments and abilities to lay claim to them openly and honestly.

Build relationships as you get visible

Self-promotion at work is fundamentally about building relationships with people. This used to make me feel stuck. How was I supposed to build a relationship with a crotchety senior man? Or how could I breeze in and say, 'I want to give you an update'? Engaging as people who share the experience of working for the same organisation makes relationship-building easier.

In psychology, the term '**confirmation bias**' is defined as the tendency to search for or interpret information in a way that confirms our personal preconceptions, while giving less consideration to alternative possibilities. According to a University of North Carolina Kenan Flagler Business School study, 'Unconscious bias is the result of the brain's lightning speed in taking in, tagging, and sorting information.' Building positive, productive relationships can be mutually beneficial in helping to avoid snap judgements in the workplace. Positive relationships can turn around hardwired preconceived ideas.

Instead of thinking of a senior leader as the older person down the hall, think of them first as a person. What's interesting about them? Now, you're back to 'curiosity' on the Mood Elevator rather than fear or discomfort. Take time to build a relationship with them before scheduling a time to meet, so you can provide an update on your work as well as ask for advice.

It's not bragging, it's education

Putting the relationship first will make your conversations easier. Once I had built a pleasant relationship with a senior leader to whom I wanted to make my work visible, it was easy to say, 'I'd love to give you an update and ask for your advice.'

People love being asked for advice. They also like 'supporting what they help build'. That includes you. If you make a senior leader feel like he or she has helped you, built you up and given you valuable advice to help your career, you are much more likely to get their ongoing support.

To give the right impression, the next step is to make sure the senior knows he or she has supported you in a positive way. They should know you've listened and that you're grateful for their advice and mentoring. One way to solidify this is to send a thank you email or note and let them know how you're using the help they provided.

Again, you aren't selling. You're building relationships, educating, getting advice and making your work visible. As Mohr says: 'What's been helpful for me...is to not think of self-promotion as pumping yourself up, faking or striving to prove anything. Instead, it can be more of a centered, honest sharing, highlighting what you've accomplished.'

Getting visible without bragging

Boasting with examples of how fabulous I was didn't feel authentic or the right action to help me get what I wanted. Instead, I worked at communicating in educational and concrete terms, with statements like:

- 'While leading the team, I was able to...'
- 'One way it's worked for me is...'
- 'I would enjoy having a more pivotal role in...'
- 'I'm confident I have the skills and experience for...'

The examples above are ways of talking objectively while still making your point. It's evident what you have accomplished without it coming across as bragging. You sound authoritative and, as a result, you'll be perceived as objective, and as if you're simply sharing good news.

Barbara J Krumsiek, Member of the Board of Directors at Arabesque Asset Management, also thinks avoiding 'trial by error' is a 'career roadblock' for many women. She believes instead of dwelling on our weaknesses, which can lead to failure, we should be more vocal about our strengths.

'I think it's important for women to respect their resumes,' she was quoted as saying in Selena Rezvani's book, *Pushback: How smart women ask – and stand up – for what they want.* 'I will try to weave into a conversation that I have math degrees or that I served on a national development team, for example...This is something we need to do skilfully; it's not merely reciting our credentials and it's not bragging either.'

Leverage your three networks

As a professional woman, you have three networks, even if you're not aware of them. The three networks you need to succeed in are your:

- Operational network

- Strategic network

- External network

The people you work with most of the time are your operational network. These are the people you need to influence to get support for projects, launch a report or get capital expenditures approved. They understand your value, your impact and your visible work. These people are probably the easiest to approach because you work with them every day. Leverage in your operational network looks like educating them on your results. Conversational openers include:

- 'Have you seen the latest ... '

- 'We're doing great. We're close to our next competitor.'

Communicating this way helps your operational network know how well your project is doing and generally what's happening.

Often there are a few minutes at the beginning of a meeting or the end, when people hang around before bolting back to their busy schedules. They might be happy to engage in a brief chat if you have a nugget of valuable information you can share, or a question you can ask. Say something like:

- 'Since you're here, I wanted to mention...'

- 'I'll be coming to you for your approval on...'

- 'The latest research is out, and the results are awesome.'

Your strategic network can help you get promoted into your next role if you educate them. They're the people within your organisation who will raise your profile once they know about you. The best practices for dealing with your strategic network will be discussed in Chapter 7, Influencing Skills.

External networks are those people outside your organisation who can help build your stature industry-wide.

It's always worth joining industry professional associations. Groups that support women like Women in Advertising, Women in Healthcare or Women in Technology can be an effective way to become known, which may be helpful when you're ready to look for another job. Participating regularly and volunteering on a project so you can meet people in your industry can be a real boon. Engaging in external networks will help you gather information, get support, gain resources and become known. You can find mentors, learn about potential openings, and talk to people about your career aspirations.

Industry-specific events are more worthwhile than general networking events that attract many entrepreneurs. While interesting to talk with, they may not be useful to your career or next position. Industry events often feature a conference with speakers, lectures on industry trends, a chat with a senior leader, or a charity fundraiser. These events are a smart place to volunteer because you're working alongside people in your industry. You may be able to serve on a committee and get to know influential people. Volunteer to organise an event if it's manageable for you.

If you're managing a lot of responsibilities inside and outside of work and feeling overwhelmed, I suggest volunteering only for a specific project, especially one where you can shine. If you have more time, then volunteer more. This can be especially worthwhile if you're looking for another job. Knowing someone who works at another company in your industry will give you an opportunity to ask questions about the business. When you go for an interview, you can be ahead of others because you'll have a better understanding of the company, the culture, and what they want.

Don't let your inner critic hold you back

As I discussed earlier, the constant, negative monkey chatter or inner critic in our minds makes us feel uncomfortable about self-promoting. Deep inside, you know self-promotion will probably work. But you may not feel you're worthy. Or you may be hesitant to take the next step. You want to be good and be liked, but you may feel you risk being judged by pushing yourself forward.

An important change for me was shifting my approach away from, 'What can I get?' toward, 'How can I help?' Highly effective networking is about helping people and connecting. When you need help later, you'll have built sweat equity and can reach back into your network and ask if they can help you.

'I'm fine, thanks' is a missed opportunity

Finally, imagine that you meet a senior leader in the corridor. You step into the same elevator and he or she says, 'Hi, Lisa. How are you?'

This is your moment. The last thing you want to do is deflect the question and turn it around. Resist the temptation to reply, 'I'm fine, how are you?' If you do that, you will miss a big opportunity to make your work visible.

Instead reply with, 'I'm great. I'm working on ... ' Then finish the sentence.

More specifically, you can say, 'I'm great. I'm working on the xxx project and we launch in December. It's been a ton of work but it's amazing and will make an incredible impact on the market.'

Lisa is no longer just sweet and nice. Instead, Lisa's working on the xxx project launching in December, and it's going to make a big impact on the market. Lisa's making important things happen. Lisa's memorable.

Another way to build your muscle for getting visible is to prepare a couple of talking points in advance. These are twenty to thirty seconds of valuable information you convey when you meet a senior leader or anyone you want to educate about what you're doing, your successes and how you're making a difference.

Once you get in the habit of doing it, you'll have your talking points ready if you see someone coming down the corridor or get chatting to them before a meeting starts. You won't deflect anymore because you'll have a few personal branding and reputation-building ideas at the tip of your tongue.

SIX

Leadership Presence And Impact

When you walk into a meeting, do you exude leadership presence? What kind of impact do you make? Are you calm, cool, present, well-put-together and in control? Or do you blast in like a whirling dervish, hair flying and ten minutes late – adding chaos and frenzy to the event?

In Chapter 3, I discussed feeling confident on the inside. In this chapter, we'll focus on what you can do to appear confident on the outside.

Appear confident even if you don't feel it

Leadership presence is the ability to project confidence, poise under pressure, gravitas and calm decisiveness.

You probably don't feel that way all the time. There are moments when you'll need to 'act as if' until your confidence work on the inside takes hold. It's OK to 'practise the future' and step into the confident, successful person you want to be and act confident until you authentically feel it.

Leadership presence is almost a subset of personal branding. It matters, because to be perceived as a woman with leadership potential, it's essential to be seen as a person capable of moving up.

Even if you don't feel confident inside, there are tactics you can implement to immediately give you the appearance of being poised and self-assured. From your body language to your tone of voice, word choices, apparel choices, handshake and energy level, you can radiate confidence outwardly, so you're perceived as a woman who belongs as leader in your organisation.

According to a 2012 study by the Center for Talent Innovation, a research organisation in New York, being *perceived* as leadership material is essential to being promoted into senior roles. The 268 senior executives who participated in this study said 'executive presence' counts for 26% of what it takes to be promoted.

A University of California study of more than 500 students, academics, and workers, published in the *Journal of Personality and Social Psychology* in 2012, showed those who appear confident achieve a higher social status. At work, these individuals tend to be more admired, listened to, and have more sway over group decisions.

Professor Cameron Anderson, who led the research, said as a result, 'Incompetent people are often promoted over their more competent peers. Displays of confidence are given an inordinate amount of weight.'

Use positive, open body language

How you dress makes an impact and telegraphs positively or negatively to others. How you use your body also displays confidence and makes you appear more powerful. Certain body postures are perceived as positive and authoritative while others are seen as hesitant or lacking in confidence.

Amy Cuddy, author of the 2015 book, *Presence: Bringing your boldest self to your biggest challenges* says:

'When our body language is confident and open, other people respond in kind, unconsciously reinforcing not only their perception of us but also our perception of ourselves. Presence emerges when we feel personally powerful, which allows us to be acutely attuned to our most sincere selves.'

While there are many details and nuances experts look for in our body language, I only want to address your vertical and horizontal axes, which indicate power and status.

Your vertical axis refers to how you take up space vertically. The taller you appear, the more you're perceived as powerful. You maximise your power with your vertical axis by standing or sitting up as straight as possible. Raising your height has the non-verbal impact of making you appear as if you have a higher status or position. Stand to your full height without slouching.

In contrast, your horizontal axis refers to taking up more space from side to side by keeping your elbows bent or gesturing widely as you speak. The more space you take from right to left is indicative of your status. Hold your arms wide as you gesture and use your hands on the table.

If you take notes in a meeting, do it so that you don't appear small. Many women hunch over their notes and take up as little space as possible, which is exactly what you shouldn't do. Don't crouch, collapse or give away your status. Jot down important items, but if you take copious notes, you'll look like an administrative assistant. While taking notes, keep your body language open and confident. I hold a wide, tall, open posture when taking notes. Remember, the taller you appear, the more status is inferred. Use your vertical space and sit tall. If you're speaking, standing up gives you more status.

Confident men often exhibit a more open body stance. Think of the term 'manspreading', sitting with the legs open. It signals power. Think about how you sit at a table. If you reduce your height and width by crossing your legs, crossing your arms, hunching your shoulders, and using a tiny space for your materials, you'll look less powerful.

Imagine you're at the front of the room. Many women cross their legs at their ankles when standing at the front of a room which reduces their horizontal axis. Then they turn their body at an angle away from their audience. Again, this reduces their horizontal space and they look smaller, which isn't a powerful pose. To be perceived as confident, sit or stand powerfully; face the room and take up space both horizontally and vertically. Plant your feet hip width apart so you appear grounded and stable.

Where you're at on the Mood Elevator will also impact your body language. On a day when you're in a low place, this may result in slumping. If you're angry, you might look like you're ready to attack. Consciously try to observe yourself from the balcony and remain 'curious' or in an even higher emotional state.

Review where you are on the spectrum for open versus closed body language in the work environment. Do you exhibit low-power poses or high-power ones? Try adjusting how you stand and sit so you appear more open, powerful and confident.

Project gravitas and a sense of importance

The word 'gravitas' refers to an air of dignity, solemnity of manner and decisiveness, which is appreciated in leaders.

Gravitas blunders, according to Sylvia Ann Hewlett, include sexual impropriety, a lack of integrity, lack of impact, inflated ego, bullying and inappropriate jokes. Someone who possesses gravitas understands the consequences of being flippant. They give the impression that they carefully consider issues and questions. They have the air of a person who's senior in experience, even if they're not.

If you're feeling or acting excited or nervous and fidgety, take a deep, clearing breath. The energy you bring into a room should be grounded, calm, positive and business-like. Make sure you're not giving off giggly, flighty, unstructured energy. Bring gravitas and structured energy. You can be positive or upbeat, but don't differ your energy too much from the others around you.

Strong, straightforward eye contact also gives the appearance of gravitas and confidence. If you struggle with eye contact, have an eye contact strategy as discussed earlier. Think of who you'll look at in a meeting. Be careful, because if you only look at the person in charge and ignore another key person, they may become irritated. Share eye contact between leaders and the person speaking. Deliberately consider who you'll maintain eye contact with, so you're not looking away, looking at your notes, or looking off in the distance. Device checking and poor eye contact indicate a lack of engagement and confidence.

SEVEN

Influencing Skills

The KPMG Leadership Study, conducted by independent research firm Ipsos, surveyed over 3,000 professional women and women college students in 2015. Among the responses given, 86% said it was important to 'be nice to others', 85% of respondents said it was important to be respectful to people in positions of authority, and 59% said they found it difficult to see themselves as a leader. Persuading and influencing may not feel comfortable, but if you're dedicated to growing, contributing more and being viewed as a leader, it's critical. In this chapter, I discuss three essential unwritten rules for you to use in a way that works best for you.

Understand why influencing skills are essential

During the early years of your career, you're rewarded for being an individual contributor, thinking of ideas and completing tasks. As you grow and become a leader, there's a change which is so imperceptible, many professionals are completely unaware of it. You don't necessarily do all the work any longer. Your team is doing some of it, under your direction. You now succeed as your team succeeds.

As the years unfold, there's another level of growth as you become more senior. Your ability to influence becomes key to your continued growth. Marshall Goldsmith, author of *What Got You Here Won't Get You There* agrees. He says, 'What brought you success in the early stages of your career regarding your ability to complete a task and do a good job becomes less important. Successful people become leaders when they shift the focus from themselves to others.'

For years, I didn't understand there was a change in what I needed to do. That was entirely unwritten and undiscovered for me.

Instead of embracing the idea of influencing, I resented having to use influencing skills and managing stakeholders because it made me uncomfortable. I was busy, and I viewed it as a huge waste of time. Surely if I did good work, it would speak for itself. I was wrong. You can influence far more effectively if you think it through strategically, map it out and act.

On several occasions over the years, I thought I could walk into a meeting without doing any influencing beforehand. I imagined myself impressing everyone with my wonderful idea and polished presentation skills, and my proposal would be considered and approved. The results were sometimes horrible. I didn't realise the real 'meeting' happens beforehand.

Through trial and error, I discovered the best way to influence others is by using a four-step approach. I share this when conducting corporate training and when working with my executive coaching clients. The four steps are:

- Use facts

- Listen and demonstrate listening

- Look for win–win

- Seek a higher purpose

Use facts to influence fact-oriented people

I tend to be a feelings-driven person, but using facts as well as feelings is most effective when influencing people. Feelings naturally help you describe an issue, a problem and its solution in an emotionally compelling way. But few people resonate with feelings alone. Include both facts and feelings while being sensitive to what the person you're trying to influence prefers. You'll need both, so bend your presentation one way or the other depending on who'll make the final decision. If you talk with a broad audience, you will especially need both facts and feelings, particularly if you want agreement or consensus on the feelings. Facts anchor you in reality. Different people respond to different information and being anchored in facts gives you a solid foundation from which to work.

Listening supports your ability to influence

The most important thing you can do to influence a person is to listen to them. Get curious so you hear not just their words, but their true concerns.

One of my clients, Jessica, was meeting with a leader who wanted to drive a big, profit-focused change in the organisation. Bill was getting some resistance and he wasn't slowing down or listening to anyone. Jessica was advocating something that didn't match what Bill wanted. His pushing seemed to have the opposite effect on people. He was shutting people down and making them feel defensive.

I described to Jessica how to listen to Bill in a deeper way and probe for the truth. Listening on the surface is one layer of listening, but often isn't enough to learn a person's real concerns. You may need to listen several layers down. Here's what this kind of listening looks like:

First, Jessica asked Bill why this change was so important to him. He replied, 'Well it's important we make more profit this year.'

She nodded and probed down to another layer of truth. 'Tell me more. Why is it important we make more profit this year?'

'Because I'm concerned if this division doesn't make more profit we won't be seen as strategic and we'll suffer as a division.'

Jessica knew, based on what I had shared with her, there might be another layer he hadn't yet revealed. Again, she asked, 'Why is it important and what does it mean for us? Tell me more.'

Bill sighed and acknowledged, 'I missed my numbers last year. If I miss my numbers again, I'm not sure I'll still have a job.'

By probing and listening three layers down, Jessica finally uncovered the truth. She got to the bottom of why Bill was pushing so strongly, disagreeing with smart people and making them feel defensive. She took her time, got curious and got into his world.

The second part of listening, which can be even more important than probing, is demonstrating you've listened. People long to feel they've been heard. People often interrupt a person they're supposed to be listening to with, 'I understand. But...' The other person doesn't feel listened to or heard when this happens.

You may think you're listening while saying something like, 'I got it. I hear you. I think...' This also doesn't demonstrate listening. People who truly listen are incredibly rare. When you talk with a person but you didn't truly hear them, the net result is ineffective and unproductive. Show you're listening by giving your full attention and reflecting back what is said.

Articulate their concerns to them as Jessica did: 'What I'm hearing you say, Bill, is you're concerned about this year's results because of last year's numbers. Am I hearing you?' She demonstrated listening by reflecting what she heard Bill say.

What you'll get in reply is often a sigh of relief because the person finally feels heard. You now have a deeper understanding of each other and your concerns. From there you can build a solution.

Create win–win solutions to influence people

Once the other person feels heard, you have a place from which to solve your differences. You understand the other person's world and why they're struggling.

Jessica was able to create a win–win solution with Bill so both could achieve what they wanted. She said, 'You're concerned with my proposal for investing in people and now I understand why you're concerned. What if we found a way to invest in people that won't impact the bottom line? Perhaps we can find a way to increase sales? Maybe we can cut something from somewhere else. Or we can schedule the training for next year. It's scheduled for January, so the money doesn't need to be paid until next year.'

David Bradford and Allan Cohen, authors of *Influence Without Authority*, say, 'Getting things done requires collaboration, and convincing others to contribute requires political skill. You get what you need by offering something of value in return.' So if you want something done, then knowing what the other person values and giving it to them can help make the situation win–win for you both.

Start from the assumption that everyone is your ally and wants a win–win solution, unless you have evidence to the contrary. Most people want to help if they see a benefit. If they don't see a benefit, it may be more challenging. If I do something for you, you're likely to feel you want to do something for me.

Consider what might be a reciprocal win for the person whose help you need. Identify something of value that you can offer before asking for assistance. Everyone has potential to be on your side if you can find a way to negotiate with them and give them what they want. What's a win, or of value to them? Do you have access to resources, important contacts, or senior leaders they might appreciate?

Maybe they're willing to help because the cause is right. Money or tools to help them do their job might motivate them to help. Would he or she like to present to the board with you? A co-worker or team member may help if they know they will get visibility in return. Or they might want something like a day off which provides more freedom. By talking about it instead of guessing, you may reveal important needs or wants not easily seen on the surface. If necessary, listen three layers down, as Jessica did with Bill.

Link the reasons why to a higher purpose

It's rare for people to genuinely do something malicious. Usually their actions are centred on their own reasons. Their mindset simply isn't synchronised with yours.

When two people argue, they often forget to look for what they can agree upon, and what they both want to accomplish. Jessica linked to a higher purpose with Bill by saying, 'I believe we should do this because you've said so often how important people are to our business. You've mentioned many times our success truly springs from our people. We both passionately believe that, don't we?'

Remind the person you're influencing that both parties are dedicated to a successful outcome to the issue. For example, 'We both want this to be an amazing launch. How can we work together to do that?' When you approach a difference of opinion this way, you're more likely to influence the other person and get what you want.

The four-step system for influencing is incredibly useful if you're preparing a big proposal, project or launch. There are other things you can do to communicate powerfully and encourage people to go along with what you want on a daily basis.

See complaints as unexpressed expectations

In almost every situation when people complain they're sharing an unexpressed expectation. Once you recognise this, you have an opportunity to turn a complaint into a win–win.

I'll use a simple example you can probably relate to at home. It's the basic question of who takes out the trash.

Do you have an agreement for who takes out the bins at your home? If you find yourself complaining your spouse or partner isn't taking out the trash, it probably means you have an unmet expectation about who is supposed to handle it. What expectation have you expressed about it?

You might be amazed how often people have expectations they've never communicated. They think the other person should magically know what they want. Is that working for you? If it's not working, then apparently mental telepathy or intuition isn't one of their core skills.

If you realise your complaint is an unmet expectation you haven't shared, you can communicate it in the form of an agreement. Say, 'My expectation is you'll do this, and I'll do that. Can we agree?' There's no emotion involved – the agreement is simple and clear.

An example from the office might be: 'Can we agree that next time, the slides will be printed out and waiting on the desk thirty minutes before the client arrives?'

Influence comes from both people knowing there's no more guessing about who does what. The other person is clear and you both sign up to follow the agreement. When you both agree to a clearly expressed expectation, it has more impact if the other person doesn't follow through.

There'd be no need to complain the slides weren't ready and the room wasn't prepared. Instead you would say, 'Susan, we agreed to that, didn't we? We agreed the meeting room and slides would be ready thirty minutes beforehand. Can you help me understand why it wasn't done?'

Women tend to have more challenges asking for what they want. I'm often asked to teach them how to do this because we don't know how to do it well. Most women fear others will think we're pushy, demanding or will be turned down, so why ask in the first place? This is a powerful way to hold people accountable and get work done.

Use influencing skills to get your next promotion

What's the difference between stakeholder management and influencing? Stakeholder management refers to the careful preparation of enhancing relationships for the most positive outcome, and it uses influencing skills. This strategy is one I've shared with many clients to help them justify their next promotion.

Make a list of all the people who'll be in the room or who'll be consulted when your next role will be discussed with Human Resources. Who'll be asked for their opinion about you? What does that list of people look like?

Then ask yourself, 'What does each person know about what I want to do?' Let them know what you want, how you're contributing and making a difference. Otherwise, they might make incorrect assumptions.

Look at your list of names and ask yourself what each of these people currently think of you. There's likely to be someone of whom you think, 'But we disagree all the time!' When it comes to your next promotion, if they're in the room, they'll probably not be a supporter. They're classified as a 'red'.

Someone you don't know will also be in the room. This person is classified as a 'yellow'. If the head of one department is someone you truly click with and you have a good relationship with them, they will support and advocate for you and so they are listed as 'green'.

Evaluate the reds, yellows and greens on your list. Would you like to shift the reds and yellows closer to green? What can you do about this? How you can fix the situation in your favour? Maybe you can put a little effort into getting to know the reds and yellows on your list. If they don't work near you but you get a chance to travel near them, consider stopping in to meet up with someone who's a yellow or a red and give them an update. Or place a call and ask your boss to set up a meeting where you can connect and build a positive relationship. Then, when you're discussed in that all-important meeting with Human Resources, you'll have more green and yellow supporters in the room and fewer reds to hold you back.

Perhaps you're about to make a big proposal and ask for a million dollars for a new piece of equipment or to fund a project. Who are the stakeholders who need to be on board? Who'll be asked for their opinion? Who'll need to say 'yes'?

If some stakeholders are people you've never met and a red or yellow, don't leave it to chance. Don't show off your amazing idea for the first time in the meeting. You'll likely meet closed doors rather than open ones. This is not the best way to accomplish things or an effective way to influence people. Go to each person and talk with them. It's like being a lobbyist who needs to convince members of parliament to vote their way.

I used to think if I built a strong proposal and presented it well, I'd be OK. I figured that facts and a smart business plan would suffice. That's not enough. Make sure you warm up everyone before the meeting. This is my approach to helping women build influencing skills and think more broadly. I enjoy helping them understand how much these steps matter, and similarly, you could share this planning approach with others too.

You may have a cutting-edge project or idea, but without effective influencing skills, you're likely be stopped cold. People aren't always promoted or passed over based on their merits alone. Valuable projects, ideas or innovations also don't always succeed or fail solely on their benefits. When you take the time to influence stakeholders, so they get to know you and understand the value of what you want to accomplish, you're far more likely to get a 'yes' vote when it truly counts.

Influencing is the key leadership skill of persuading others to go along with what you believe is best. Along the way, you may compromise, but it's an important part of leadership. The ability to bring a mindful approach to influencing and to do it effectively will make a huge difference to your career.

EIGHT
Difficult Conversations

In the heat of a disagreement, it's easy to focus on our differences. But it's more useful to focus on what we agree upon. In this chapter, we'll explore difficult conversations and conflict in the workplace as well as the unwritten rules to resolve it. People at work aren't always calm, measured and professional in tone. When you don't know what to do or how to handle it when someone gets upset, pain is often the result. Those were some of the times I ended up crying silently in the ladies'. I'll discuss how to bring the flames down to a simmer, manage it, and find a way to use it for good by dissipating an argument and coming to a workable solution.

The possibility of conflict was a source of pain for me early on. Raised in a home with few disagreements,

I mistakenly made disagreement at work about me, not the issue. As you can tell, I was a 'conflict avoider'. If you disagreed with me, it meant our relationship was unravelling and we couldn't be friends. When I finally learned to separate the relationship from the disagreement, I could have healthy disagreements, remain friends, and get to the truth.

Keep in mind that, when it comes to conflict at work, women are held to a different standard. Women tend to be seen differently from men when dealing with conflict, too. If a man comes down hard for an idea or a policy, everyone says, 'Wow, he's strong. What a hard-charger.' But if a woman reacts the same way, the team might say, 'What a bitch!'

Conflict can be a good thing

Conflict isn't always personal, nor is it always negative. Conflict can be a good thing when it's done well and you recognise it's not about you.

Most people aren't taught to manage conflict. As a result, how you have seen conflict in the world and in your family has probably shaped your beliefs about how to handle it. There's a good way to disagree with others so you're clear and accomplish your aims. There's also a way to disagree which results in stalemates and hurt feelings. Most people handle conflict poorly. You may have grown up with the impression that conflict and difficult conversations are bad and to be avoided at all costs. When it's done well, though, conflict can be a catalyst to move things forward.

Learning to reframe conflict in a healthier, more open-minded context was a game-changer for me. If you're angry or upset, that won't help. Staying emotionally clear as you discuss matters, and encouraging others to stay in a healthy, open place is the best way. When you look at where you're at on the Mood Elevator, if your conversation is making you frustrated, afraid or angry, do your best to come back to a place of 'curious' again. Say to yourself, 'Wow! This is getting interesting.' Ask questions like:

- 'Why do they feel this way?'

- 'I wonder why they're so upset?'

- 'How can I help?'

- 'Where should we go from here?'

- 'What can we agree upon?'

Returning to being curious will help you stop yourself before you get angry or overly emotional. Rather than escalating a difficult conversation into a conflict, look at your discussion from the vantage point of 10,000 feet up in the air in a helicopter, and respond from a considered place that shows you're listening.

Determine what kind of disagreement you're having

If you do some detective work as you talk to the person you're in conflict with, your investigation will lead to greater understanding and bring you to a better solution. If you just disagree and dig your heels in, you may be left with limited options.

Amy Gallo, author of the *HBR Guide to Dealing with Conflict* suggests you slow down and first consider what the disagreement is truly about. Most disagreements are either about tasks, processes, relationships or status. Here are examples of all four:

- **Task** conversations are about how and when a task is completed

- **Process** arguments are about what procedure should be used

- **Relationship** arguments happen when a relationship is called into question

- **Status** arguments are about who should make a decision

Taking a moment to reflect on which of these are under discussion can help you separate what you do agree on and what needs to be resolved. Where is the disagreement or point of friction? Come up with a clear question about what everyone's trying to accomplish.

Do we want to spend the money? Do we agree on this course of action? Even if there's noise in the room, understanding is crucial. Perhaps we agree about spending the money, but don't agree yet how to do it.

Another point of disagreement may be around status and who decides. Is it my decision to spend the money, or is it yours? Clarifying who's in charge may de-escalate the situation.

Finally, summarise what you've agreed on by saying something like, 'I hear us agreeing this paper should go to the board and we should ask for the funding. Do we agree on those terms?' This confirmation may depersonalise any remaining conflict, whether real or perceived, allowing you to move forward.

Recognise people with different conflict styles

We will encounter people who shout or become difficult. It's important to realise we're not the only person they're difficult with. Their combative style is how they deal with differences.

Knowing this helped me notice how I used to make conflicts about me because I felt I wasn't good enough. However, I learned that if I tried to listen instead to what was being said by the other person, rather than their personal style of delivery, then I could stay engaged much more effectively. I remind myself that that's probably how communication happened in their family, and naturally it became their style. It may take a lot to push past the delivery, listen and depersonalise the message. But then you can determine what you can agree upon and arrive at a point where you can have a fruitful, productive conversation. Back when I personalised these conversations, I felt there had to be a winner and a loser. I didn't want to lose, so I felt I must say something to get the upper hand, which often didn't work.

Conflict avoiders will often disengage from a difficult conversation. They want to remove themselves from conflict at almost all costs. They may fidget, be slow to respond, or act in a passive-aggressive manner. Conflict seekers want to be right. They believe they're being direct and honest. They're unworried about ruffling feathers and will get into a heated discussion in the interest of getting things done.

If you tend to be a conflict avoider, step up and be willing to have difficult conversations with grace and ease. Realise conflict can be a good thing and can bring you to a better solution. It doesn't necessarily mean the relationship is unravelling.

If you're a conflict seeker, let it go more often. Resist the temptation to win. Listen to the other person and consider how you could be contributing to the problem. The goal isn't to be right, it's to come to agreement.

Do you want to be right or do you want to be happy? Remember that you may have a different conflict style at work compared to at home.

Using the tools of influence, depersonalising and calmly dealing with people who have a high tolerance for conflict removes the idea of win–lose. The conversation shifts to win–win, which is more positive and works for both parties.

Separate the delivery from the substance

There can be a huge difference between what someone says and the tone in which they say it. If someone snaps at you, it can shake you up and be unnerving. Your instant reaction may be, 'Wow, what a jerk!' or, 'How dare he talk to me that way!' Separate yourself from the emotion and delivery and focus on the message. How it was delivered has nothing to do with you.

Marshall Goldsmith says our background and genetics are the reasons why some people stay calm and others anger quickly. He says, 'If you had their background, genetics and upbringing you'd probably act that way, too.'

In Chapter 2 on Self-leadership, I explained when you take things personally, your initial reaction may be to shut down or feel defensive. However, beneath all the bluster, there's probably something important being said. Once you look for the kernel of truth amid the angry words, ask how you can own your part. Can you take responsibility for what you can both agree on? For example, you could say, 'We both agree we want to get this project done. How can we move forward together?'

In the moment of conflict, you have a choice in how you respond. Depending on your conflict style and your comfort level with conflict, you may say, 'Let's not go down that road.' When you're faced with a difficult conversation and you feel triggered by how someone speaks, there's a moment where you can choose to escalate the situation or defuse it. People who handle conflict poorly react from their gut and escalate the situation, rather than respond thoughtfully.

Should you avoid conflict by being relentlessly nice? No. Being 'too nice' and avoiding difficult but necessary conversations isn't the answer. You can be candid, honest and still respectful. You can stay in your power and deliver a strong, difficult message in a kind way. Depersonalising things by being curious or by finding where you can agree de-escalates a situation. You might think it feels unjust, and you may be right. But someone must be the grown-up in the room.

Many behavioural experts say the only emotion men feel 'allowed' to express is anger. Often they don't feel able to express their full range of emotions and fighting fire with fire doesn't work. It only makes the situation worse. You can react unconsciously with anger and righteous indignation about how you've been wronged or insulted. Or you can take a moment and respond differently, which will de-escalate and depersonalise the situation, and bring it back to where positive solutions are possible.

Even in conflict, look for win–win solutions

Even when you're in conflict, look for ways to uncover those win–win solutions and a higher purpose for what you're doing. Ask questions like:

- What do I want from this conversation?

- What are my goals?

- What do they want?

Be brutally honest with yourself and make certain you're not arguing simply because you want to be right. Focus on solutions rather than who's right.

Achieving a win–win solution means you both may need to compromise. Or the other person's solutions could truly be the best way forward. Insisting your outcome needs to look a certain way or be what you want may not end up being a win–win.

If necessary, take a break

Maintaining composure is important. However, you don't need to sit there and be verbally abused. You can step away and say, 'This doesn't feel constructive.' Then take a break and come back in five minutes. Or say, 'Let's have this conversation when we're both calm.' If you're not running the meeting, calling for a break may seem a bit impertinent, but you could say you are going to get another cup of coffee and take a few moments to regain your composure.

A break also allows the other person to quietly compose his or her thoughts. When you return in five minutes, the situation may still be unacceptable in their mind, but they too will have had a breather to think things through. Some people are comfortable expressing conflict and need to vent before they calm down. This can help them communicate their message in a more constructive, effective way.

Amy Cuddy says in *Presence: Bringing your boldest self to your biggest challenges* that there are four choices in the face of conflict:

- Just be nice and ignore it. Ignore the fact they were rude to you.

- Deal with it in an indirect, passive-aggressive way by complaining about it behind their back. (Cuddy doesn't recommend this approach.)

- Deal with the problem constructively and directly.

- Leave. This could be temporarily, such as by taking time away, or permanently, by asking to work with a different team.

Later you can come to an agreement about how both of you will behave and put healthy boundaries around how you speak to each other. You might say, 'I don't respond well to being shouted at. It's not the most effective way for us to work together. Can we agree we will speak calmly?'

Be willing to have difficult conversations

If you're as uncomfortable with conflict as I was, you can probably feel it coming on. Instead of shutting down or getting defensive, though, remember how easy it can be to slide down in the Mood Elevator. If you don't initiate a difficult conversation now, it may return later as conflict. Being nice because you don't want to upset the balance is a strategy that may blow up in your face further down the line.

One of my clients, Marisa, was a conflict avoider. Her boss was also an avoider. When she started working for her company, she was given vague promises that she'd be promoted to a certain level. Yet her boss avoided conversations with her about what she needed to do to move to the next level. She wanted to talk about her goals and what she needed to get promoted. The impact on her was that she felt demotivated because he didn't take his promise seriously, and her career wasn't moving forward.

I helped Marisa get her boss to discuss his promises and how he always cancelled meetings or changed the subject. Instead of avoiding the difficult conversation, she got him back on track to help her grow and contribute more. He didn't realise the impact his actions had had on her. He was busy in his world and didn't notice her frustration. She was promoted and is now a senior manager.

The best way to have a difficult conversation is by using the following process:

- Explain your circumstances or situation and how it impacts you

- Ask for what you want different from the other person

- Get an agreement from the other person about how to resolve the problem

NINE

Negotiating Strategies

Unfortunately, most books written about negotiating were written by and for men. The reasons why you should negotiate are rock solid. However, the strategies in most of these books don't always work for women.

Negotiate your starting salary

Monica accepted her current position because she hated her previous job. She didn't negotiate her starting salary when she was hired because she was desperate to get out of her old company. As a result, she started near the bottom of the pay grade and only made small, incremental gains. When she came to me, I encouraged her to find mentors, which you'll read more about in Chapter 11. One mentor she chose was a more senior man in her company.

As part of their mentoring discussion, he asked how much she was paid. He replied, 'Do you know you're being underpaid? Go back and ask for a pay rise.'

She went to Human Resources and said, 'I understand what the salary range is for my position. I'm a high-level performer and I think I'm being underpaid.'

They agreed, and she received a $30,000 a year pay rise. She admitted that she never would have asked if her mentor hadn't challenged her to do so.

In *Women Don't Ask* by Linda Babcock and Sara Laschever, Linda discusses that when she was director of a PhD program a group of women students complained that they weren't being given the same opportunities to teach as the male students: 'She asked the associate dean...about it. She received a simple answer. He explained, "More men ask. The women just don't ask."'

A 2010 study reported in the *Journal of Personality and Social Psychology* revealed males graduating from MBA programs negotiated their salary half the time. Women MBA graduates negotiated only one-eighth of the time. The authors of the study noted negotiation is particularly intimidating to women, because the language required is inconsistent with what is considered to be polite for a woman to say.

I learned the importance of negotiating successfully as a woman later in my career. Several years after college, I realised I never negotiated my starting salary. When

I was offered my first job, negotiating my salary never occurred to me. I was so grateful to be offered a job at top company, I didn't consider it.

Your starting salary in your first job sets a financial trajectory for your entire career. Let's say you're a graduate aged twenty-two or twenty-three and you accept an entry-level position at $50,000 per year. On the same day, a man is offered the same job at the same starting salary. He negotiates and starts at $60,000 per year. In our example, he only negotiates once, but over the years, this still makes a massive difference in his earnings.

Your careers each follow the same path. You both receive an annual 3% salary increase, but the woman who didn't negotiate never catches up with the man who negotiated one time, right after college. Every year, his 3% increase grows his salary faster than hers. Look at the difference in income on the table below.

	DIDN'T NEGOTIATE	DID NEGOTIATE	DIFFERENCE
Year 1:	$50,000	$60,000	$10,000
Year 5:	$56,276	$67,530	$11,254
Year 10:	$65,238	$78,286	$13,048
Year 15:	$75,630	$90,754	$15,124
Year 20:	$87,674	$105,208	$17,534
Year 25:	$101,640	$121,966	$20,326
Year 30:	$119,828	$141,392	$21,564
Totals:	$2,380,760	$2,854,480	$473,720

By the time you both reach retirement age, he's made almost half a million dollars more than you. Then add interest for investing the money over the years. If the person who negotiated invests the difference in a low yield account, at retirement age, his account will be worth $784,000 more than yours – just because he negotiated once. This example is a combination of the power of compound interest and negotiating. Even if you both receive the same annual salary increase, because he started with a higher base, he pulls ahead further every year. If you don't negotiate, you'll never catch him up.

Ask for what you want

Women rarely ask for what they want because the voices in our heads say we're not good enough or we feel guilty about asking for more. As a result, most women trust they'll receive what they want without asking for it. This is a poor formula for getting what you want. Marie C Wilson, founder of 'Take Our Daughters to Work Day' and the Foundation for Women, a White House project, said, 'Show me a woman without guilt and I'll show you a man.'

Start by deciding what you want. This happens when you know your value in the organisation and what you contribute. Make a list of your responsibilities and notable achievements. Then, know your external value – what you'd be worth at other companies. What's your market rate? What would other corporations pay you in the same city? Check on Glassdoor.com or look at online advertisements, speak to headhunters or ask your mentors. Questions you might ask include:

- What is the pay range for this level?

- What should someone in my role be paid?

- What would a man in my role be paid?

When you ask for what you want, consider the context of your negotiation:

- Who should you ask?

- When should you ask?

Timing is important. Requesting a salary increase just after budgets are set may be too late. On the opposite side of the equation, if you just had a stellar performance review, won a prize, an award, delivered a significant milestone or an impressive achievement, it may be an ideal time to ask.

In a study by Linda Babcock, seventy-four volunteers were brought into a laboratory to play a word game. Volunteers were told they would be paid anywhere from $3 to $10 for their time. After playing, each student was given $3 and asked if the sum was OK. Eight times more men than women asked for more money.

In their 2008 book, *Ask for It: How women can use the power of negotiation to get what they really want,* authors Babcock and Laschever say:

'Even when women can imagine changes which might increase their productivity at work, their happiness at home, or their overall contentment with their lives, their suppressed sense of entitlement creates real barriers to their asking. Because they're not dissatisfied with what they have and not sure they deserve more, women often settle for less.'

Everything is negotiable

When you take a new job or are moved to another city or country, Human Resources put together a salary and benefits package where they consider your new salary and the cost of living where you're going. For example, they might say, 'This is what a Marketing Director makes in New York.' Or, 'It's more expensive to live in San Francisco, so you'll get 20% more.' Most of the time when you move from one part of the country to another, you get paid the market rate for the position in that city.

The first time I moved, Human Resources took a long time preparing my package. I was getting closer to my departure date and they kept telling me they were still putting the package together. Human Resources said, 'We know everything is slow, but sign and we'll figure it out later.' I agreed, which meant I accepted the package without seeing it. I was almost on my flight to Cyprus before it arrived. Then they wouldn't negotiate because I had accepted my package when I signed. I had absolutely no bargaining power.

Next time I moved jobs, the same thing happened, but I knew better how to navigate it this time. Human Resources said, 'Just accept it and we'll figure everything out later,' but I was exceedingly gracious and said 'Absolutely, but I'd like to see the numbers first before I agree.' Eventually the numbers arrived, and I could negotiate.

I had known what to expect, so I prepared. Assume everything is negotiable and you'll be ahead, because typically women don't speak up. Before accepting, negotiate everything at once – your salary, cost of living increase, mode of travel, hotels, moving expenses, working hours, car allowance, healthcare, pension, work from home base: absolutely everything can be negotiated. Start from that perspective and go forward. Two helpful online resources include:

- Glassdoor.com, which lets you compare salaries and pay rates for different positions in different markets and at different companies.

- Numbeo.com allows you to compare the cost of living and housing prices for any two cities around the world. It also lets you compare non-financial criteria like traffic, health care, quality of life and more.

Use 'anchoring' to negotiate your salary

Over the years, I discovered a technique called 'anchoring'. Here's how it works: if we just talked about the number 16 and then I asked you to give me a number between 1 and 100, what number would you choose? Now, I ask you the same question, but this time we just talked about the number 87. What number would you choose?

The likelihood is you'll give me a higher number when we were discussing 87 compared to when we talked about 16 earlier. This principle is called anchoring. It's something our brains automatically latch onto when you put a number out there.

Using anchoring is helpful if you know the salary range. Let's say you know the salary range for a position is $80,000 to $100,000. Start by anchoring them with: 'I'm looking for in the region of $110,000.' That will anchor in the minds of the people you're negotiating with that you belong at the top of the scale. They'll still try to negotiate your salary down, and they should. If you ask for your target salary, they'll negotiate it down and you'll end up with less. Ask for a little more than your target salary. Rarely will they accept your first offer – and you shouldn't accept their first offer either.

Knowing the salary range for a position allows you the opportunity to raise their top offer. It'll also raise their perception about you and your value. If you don't know the correct salary range, you could miss out. If you don't know the range is $100,000 to $125,000 you might talk yourself out of $25,000. Remember, they need you as much as you need them. When you're at the point where they've decided you're the best person for the role, you're at the point of maximum power and absolutely should negotiate. Never accept the first offer. Always ask for more.

Leave your emotions out of negotiations

Many women imagine a salary negotiation will be a stress-filled conversation because they're uncomfortable talking about money and their worth. The entire experience risks becoming an emotionally charged one. According to Babcock and Laschever, 'When asked to pick metaphors for the process of negotiating, men picked "winning a ballgame" and "a wrestling match" while women picked "going to the dentist".'

Leave your emotions at the door and be scrupulously well-prepared. Have facts and information at your fingertips. If you know your worth, it doesn't need to be a nail-biting experience.

Mika Brzezinski, the co-host of *Morning Joe* on MSNBC and author of *Know Your Value* who made five attempts to renegotiate her salary situation but made the mistake of apologising every time said: 'I think women have a hard time not apologising their way into negotiations...

I learned to be pragmatic and dial back the emotions, because I observed men do it when they came to me for salary negotiations.'

Practise asking for what you want

If you're uncomfortable hearing the word 'no' as a professional woman, you're not negotiating enough. Get comfortable hearing it. One way to practise is to pretend you don't have enough money in the super-market, or ask for a free cup of coffee at Starbucks or a favour from a friend. Practise asking people for things, so you grow comfortable with people saying 'no'. You won't faint or die if you're turned down. Yes, it's awkward, but it will expand your comfort zone and make it easier when what you're asking for is more important than a cup of coffee.

Look for win-win opportunities

Negotiating collaboratively is critical. Coming from a win–win position is more effective than coming from win–lose. Acting as if you're holding your boss up at gunpoint doesn't work. Your approach must take into account what management wants, so view things from their perspective and solve problems for both of you. A straightforward salary request should be a simple negotiation, but be prepared for these conversations to become complex, and find a balance between firmness and flexibility.

How you ask is critical

One woman asked for what she wanted with disastrous results. Her boss pushed his chair back like he was pulling himself away – as if perhaps he had made a mistake offering her the job. In an unfriendly tone, he said, 'When we offered you this job, we thought you'd fit in well with our team-oriented style and collaborative way.'

She had stepped outside the accepted behavioural norm of being nice. Research shows that it is much less effective if women negotiate aggressively. Men can only negotiate aggressively with other men. Women are often more successful when they use a calm, powerful, win–win style. But remember, that doesn't mean you shouldn't negotiate – you absolutely must. Always. But *how* you do it makes the difference.

Babcock and Laschever suggest you make a concerted effort to focus on a win–win outcome by asking questions and soliciting feedback by saying things like:

- 'What you think we should do?'
- 'How can we fix it?'
- 'Let's work together.'
- 'Can you help me to…?'
- 'I understand that you…'
- 'My solution helps you to…'

Remind them why they hired you

Say: 'You hired me to be a capable negotiator in this role. This is the last time you and I will be on the opposite sides of the table.'

Don't say: 'I want the next job up. I've paid my dues and I deserve a promotion.'

Say: 'I want to contribute at the next level. I'm sure I could contribute more with more responsibility. I'd like an opportunity to show you how much more I can do. I would appreciate the chance to persuade you that I am the right person for the job.'

The most important thing is to take a deep breath, get out of your comfort zone and decide to negotiate. Prepare yourself to express the salary you want by knowing what your position pays and by knowing your value to the organisation. When you negotiate, do it in a way that's win–win and collaborative so you're viewed as an asset and not as difficult. This combination should gain you more respect within your company and a higher level of income.

TEN

Time Mastery

When I conduct corporate training or work with clients, one question I'm asked about more than any other is work–life balance. It's one facet of our lives that many women struggle to get right. Whether my client is constantly dealing with an onslaught of emails or trying to figure out how to squeeze in time to buy groceries, attend her daughter's football tournament and review a report before falling into bed, these are just some of the factors that detract from her achieving that all-important work–life balance.

First, I must make a key correction. The term 'work–life balance' is a misnomer. There is no such thing as 'balance', there is only 'balancing'. 'Balance' implies we can create something stationary and permanent. In fact, we'll never achieve that. Work–life 'balancing' more accurately captures how it is a dynamic, flawed and ever-changing activity. Trying to find balance every day is unrealistic. Balancing happens over months or years, and you constantly work at it as kids get sick, boilers blow up, cars need maintenance, and other things happen that make it unlikely you'll have complete balance every single day.

Who you marry is the biggest career decision you'll ever make

The person you choose as your spouse or life partner has much to do with how far you grow in your career and how you handle your life when you're not at work. If you marry someone who isn't supportive, your home life will find a way to intrude at the worst times. If it hadn't been for my husband's support throughout the years we were married, I know it would've been impossible to do many of the things I've done in my career.

I don't know a successful woman in leadership whose life partner isn't fully supportive of her career. Research indicates that with every 1-standard-deviation increase in a spouse's conscientiousness, an individual is likely to earn approximately $4,000 more per year. Being married to a conscientious spouse makes you likely to be promoted more often too. This is because aware, helpful spouses are more likely to handle household tasks, allowing their partner to focus more on their career. This doesn't mean your success depends on your being in a relationship. There are plenty of single people who shine at work, and there are plenty of effective business leaders who are unattached. But if you choose a partner, the partner you choose to share your journey with makes a big difference, in work and in life.

Don't give it all away

I learned the difference between 'giving it all' and 'giving it all away' on my journey. There's nothing wrong with giving your all and working hard. But make sure you're not giving it all away and working to the point where you don't have a life.

I coach many successful women, but some are emotionally over-invested in work. That's easy to do in your twenties. You care deeply and are working hard to make a difference and get noticed. Some of us over-commit emotionally and work to a point where we're missing from our own list of priorities.

It's a marathon, not a sprint. Many women are trying to race through their career as if they were sprinting an entire twenty-six-mile race. They're likely to burn out and eventually give up because it's impossible to maintain balance that way. Depending on what you do, there may be days that require working incredibly long hours. There may be a period in your life where you work long hours, but you can't do it forever.

I was given excellent advice one evening while at my desk late at night. It was the early days of my career and Joan was the head of market research for the company. She walked past me toiling at my desk and asked, 'Why are you still here?'

I replied, 'I'm working.'

She said, 'My advice is you don't give 110% or 120%. Give 95% and save a little for you. They'll never notice the difference.'

Your 95% is probably 100% for many other people. Remember to hold back something for yourself. It will make you a happier, less stressed person.

Let go of the guilt

There's a massive divide between working and stay-at-home mothers. Much of the divide is unspoken, but both of us carry guilt. Mothers who stay at home might not enjoy their new role as much as they thought they might, or might feel they've lost some of their independence because they no longer have an income. Mothers who work might struggle because they're constantly worried about whether their children are suffering while they are at work. They may wonder if they're being enough of a mother.

If you are a mother, get clear about your choices. Ask yourself, 'Am I a better mother if I work? Or would I be better if I stayed home?' For me, it was obvious. I was happier and more fulfilled because I worked. We also had a better quality of life because of my career. My children got to live in six countries and they enjoyed amazing experiences because I worked.

When my son Alex was in third grade, one of the working mothers I knew well was my friend Clare. We lived in Kuala Lumpur at the time. Clare's son was in Alex's class. Alex came home one day from school and said, 'Mum, Joseph and I are the two smartest kids in our class. I think it's because we have the smartest mothers because you're both working.'

I'm not sure if we were the smartest, but it was fascinating to see what he saw. He thought that I was smart, and that it was cool that his mother worked. I dropped a lot of the guilt after that, and I'm glad I did.

If you harbour guilt because you can't always be there for your children, there is encouraging news:

- When children see a strong work ethic in their mothers, it gives them a greater sense of independence and some of the problem-solving skills they'll need in the world of work.
- Author Lisa Evans says children of working mothers are more resilient and likely to bounce back from tough times better. As children reach the age where they will start making career choices, they also feel they have a wider network to tap into.

A Harvard study revealed daughters of working mothers earn up to 23% more than their counterparts whose mothers stayed at home throughout their growing up years and men raised by a working mother contribute more at home.

It doesn't matter whether you work outside the home or not; you're a role model to your children. If you're going to work, be confident and let go of any guilt. Don't be a mother who spends countless hours stricken and struggling. Your children are watching you as a mentor and role model. You wouldn't want your children to see a role model who doesn't love herself and take care of herself. Let them see their mother in a fulfilling career that she loves. That's the example our daughters and sons need.

Get help because you can't do it all

I frequently tell working mothers to get help. Obviously, the amount of help you can get is proportional to the help you need and how much you're able to pay. For women who aren't in a well-paid career, it's more difficult. I fully realise it's not fair and it's not right, but do your best to avail yourself of whatever help you can manage. Maybe you can trade with a friend, or perhaps family can help.

If you can afford it, spend the money on great childcare so that you can work without worrying about your children. To make a powerful, successful career sustainable, you must be able to focus on your work when you are at work, knowing your children are in capable hands. Get the best childcare you can and line up backup care, too. Use whatever services make sense – look online and ask for recommendations. Consider a nanny-share if that would help with logistics and finances.

Manage your boundaries

It's said, 'If you want something done, ask a busy person.' That person will probably reply with a 'yes'.

Women often have a tough time when it comes to saying 'no'. In my training sessions, I often say, 'Do you know what your inbox is? It's a list of other people's priorities for you. It's what the world wants you to do.'

What are your intentions and priorities? What are you focused on? An important part of work–life balance is to be in control of what you do.

Learn to say 'no' graciously and manage what's on your list. Don't do things because you think you should, or because it might look bad if you refuse. We often take on tasks that shouldn't be on our list. Sometimes we don't control what goes on our list at all – you'll have work delegated to you that you cannot refuse. I was extremely disciplined about where I spent time outside work and at work. I was selective, strategic and never took on projects just because someone asked.

Saying 'no' can be extremely difficult. One way to do it is to keep it simple and say, 'Thank you for asking, but this isn't going to work for me.' Or, 'I'm already booked for that timeslot.' It's easier to say you're booked when you have everything scheduled in your calendar. This includes not just all your work commitments, but also movie night with your family, workouts at the gym, date night with your spouse or partner, and anything else that matters to you.

I always consider these requests and think, 'Will this help me in any way? Will it make me happier?' If it doesn't do either, I find a polite way to refuse.

Managing two careers takes planning and compromise

In a July 2012 article of *Harvard Business Review* on 'How Two-Career Couples Stay Happy', the author shares the importance of actively managing your expectations of each other. The article recommends scheduling time with your spouse. We schedule meetings, conferences, time to complete assignments, and workouts. But most of us don't think to schedule time with our significant other. There are no perfect solutions, but you must discuss your career ambitions and decide who'll have the lead career in your marriage and when. There may be a time when the children are young when your spouse's career takes priority. Later, it can be your turn. One person shouldn't have to make all the sacrifices.

An April 2015 *Harvard Business Review* article said:

> 'Consciously or unconsciously, couples adopt *strategies* to manage the demands of each career plus a shared domestic life. There's the "one career/one job" pattern, in which the primary breadwinner's career is consistently prioritised, while the other partner's employment is made up of jobs that take lower priority.'

Setting guidelines for how you'll handle two careers could be essential for the continued success of your relationship, and your career.

Let your partner truly contribute as a partner

Many married men say they do their fair share of chores, but their wives disagree. In fact, a 2005 University of Michigan study revealed that having a husband creates an additional seven hours of housework per week for their wives. On balance, having a wife saves a man one hour of housework a week.

There's a mental load that women bear also, especially working mothers. Sometimes partnerships can be uneven. Many women will tell you their husband doesn't do his fair share and he needs to be directed. As a result, the mother is responsible not just for the parenting, but also the household duties and organising, reminding and planning social events. The mental load includes having to remember everything from when the cable guy is coming to the children's doctor appointments. The mother's mental load is exhausting and it's invisible.

Somehow women end up in the position of Chief Operating Officer of the family. When a man expects his partner or wife to ask for his help, he assumes she's responsible for everything. When she's expected to take on the task of organisation and execute a large portion of the work herself, it's not a fifty-fifty partnership.

A friend of mine told me shortly after she started living with her partner that he said: 'I better stay out of your way in the kitchen. I'm probably more of a liability than an asset.' This is what I call 'strategic incompetence'. Some men get away with doing less at home. Do you take pity on your husband and say, 'Oh, he doesn't know how to pack a lunch?' or 'He doesn't know how to do laundry'? He won't know how if you jump in and do everything. You married him because he's smart – he'll figure it out. If you let him get away with strategic incompetence, then you'll end up shouldering the load. Share the work with him and let him be involved as a real partner.

Don't be a mother who irons

If you can possibly afford it, don't be a mother who cleans the house. There are no prizes for ironing straight creases or for carrying out the white glove test.

A friend of mine told me she put herself through college years ago by cleaning homes. Once she graduated, she vowed she'd never scrub another toilet again. She finally reached a point where she could afford it. She hires someone for a few hours to clean the bathrooms, wash the floors and do a few other chores. The rest she splits with her husband.

Those who can't afford household help or childcare may find creative ways to trade chores with neighbours, friends and family members. Whatever you choose, make your overall well-being and happiness a priority. Coming home to stressed-out kids because you don't have help when you can afford it won't help you sustain your career over the years. Spending your entire weekend cleaning house won't bring you joy, peace or a closer relationship with the people you love. Get help if you can, and realise true happiness isn't found in spotless floors, polished furniture or sparkling windows.

ELEVEN

Mentors And Sponsors

We've all been told we're supposed to network and find mentors and sponsors on our journey – that wasn't an unwritten rule for me. But I didn't know who to ask or how. In my experience, older, senior men seem to spontaneously reach out to younger men, perhaps because they remind them of themselves when they were younger in their careers or because they played or follow the same sport, which creates a connection outside the office. It becomes almost like a father–son relationship.

Younger men also seem to find it easier to ask a senior man for support. They're more confident, and older men are drawn to take an interest. This opens the door for men to get together for coffee or a beer after work and have those important conversations.

Mentors and sponsors are different

Before you start looking for mentors and sponsors, it helps to understand the difference between the two. Both mentors and sponsors are career accelerators and one often naturally springs from the other. A mentor helps you accelerate because they share what they have learned, what they'd do again, what they'd avoid, and what warning signs to watch for on the path. Mentors talk *to* you about their past journeys.

In my corporate career, I worked in six countries. Having the opportunity to talk to a mentor who'd relocated their family to another country, been an expat, been through the process of getting an assignment, negotiated with Human Resources, worked with the moving company and the relocation people would have been incredibly helpful. Whether you need to know about working in finance, being a working mother, negotiating with difficult clients, or any other topic, mentors can help by sharing their experiences. They may not always get it right. But they'll provide guidance so you're not going it alone.

Not having mentors can slow you down and make the process of career progression more painful. When you're on your own and must figure out everything without support, it doesn't mean you won't succeed, but the journey is sure to be tougher.

But mentoring is different from sponsorship. Sponsors are even higher-level accelerators who know you and your work directly and are willing to advocate for you and sing your praises when it really counts. Sponsors talk *about* you when you aren't in the room. They advocate for you.

Say an Executive Vice President asks his colleagues, 'Who do we know who could take on an overseas assignment in Asia?' A sponsor will speak up and say, 'Susan's in the Middle East already. She could handle it. I think she'd be wonderful. Did you know she's already managed a whole portfolio and did a great job? She has the ability to do it again in another region.'

Sponsors are usually people you've worked for, or whom you've worked with closely. They know you and your work. After all, you wouldn't recommend a dentist you've never met. People put their reputation on the line when they sponsor you. If a sponsor says, 'Susan's ideal for the job in Asia,' and she does poorly, management will feel the sponsor got it wrong.

A 2015 study reported in the *Academy of Management Journal* and conducted by Belle Rose Ragins and John L Cotton revealed that women tend to have a more challenging time developing relationships with a mentor or sponsor compared to men. Less experienced protégés report taller barriers to obtaining a mentor. The unwritten rules I've outlined below will help you gain the benefits of support from mentors and sponsors.

Some companies have formal mentoring programmes in which you're allocated a mentor. Assigned roles work out in some cases, but in others, the relationship may feel stilted and lacking connection. I had this experience with one mentor. I felt intimidated and didn't have trust in him. It wasn't a win–win mentoring relationship. The most powerful relationships are often those you create yourself that emerge out of a natural connection between two people. Don't wait for your company to find you a mentor. If they do, that's great. But also do it yourself and build your own relationships.

Before reaching out to a mentor, clearly define what you want. If I'd known then what I know now about finding and creating mentors to help me achieve, I would have asked myself important questions about what I truly wanted from the mentorship first. Here are some questions you may want to ask yourself:

- What are the career journeys I want to go on?
- Who's walked those journeys ahead of me?
- Who can help me to figure out what I want?

These questions will help clarify your aims and point you toward mentors and sponsors who'll help you take the next steps toward your desired career direction.

At the same time, look around you and be proactive as far as other women are concerned. Is there someone who is in the same position you were in when you started whom you could be advising and supporting? Do you have specialist expertise that you could be sharing with a woman working in that area?

Choose mentors who match your career journeys

To identify a potential mentor, don't randomly select a few people who work nearby. Carefully think through which people could be most helpful to you. Work through the questions above and think through the journeys you want to take in your career. If you're in marketing and you want to advance, choosing someone who's senior to you in marketing would be a wise choice. A person who's walked that path should absolutely be one of your mentors. Because they're ahead of you, they'll probably ask you specific questions such as, have you worked:

- With a big agency?
- On a global brand?
- On a new product launch?

They'll have knowledge and experience and can provide suggestions to help you harness your career.

What other career journeys do you envision? Do you want to be an entrepreneur? Maybe you want to work in finance. Perhaps there's a company in your mind you'd like to work for, or you want to work overseas.

You may want to work in another city or state. A mentor who's worked in that city would be valuable, whether their experience is in marketing or not. My mentor Nick was a terrific help when I asked him questions like:

- How did you get on the list to go to that city?
- When did you look at schools for your kids?
- How did you introduce the idea to your spouse?

Perhaps you want to become an entrepreneur instead. A mentor who owns a business can provide helpful insight into that career path. When I decided to branch out and create Powerful Growth Group, I asked my mentor:

- How did you build a bridge between paid work and entrepreneurship?
- What type of company entity did you form?
- Can you recommend a good accountant?

I gained so much from a mentor who was also a working mum in a senior role. This type of mentor may not work in your field, for your company, or even in your industry. You can ask this mentor more personal questions such as how she:

- Handles it all when it gets to be overwhelming
- Copes with feelings of guilt
- Plans when school calls and her child is sick
- Manages a nanny or other helpers

By understanding the career journeys you want to go on, you can find someone who's ahead of you and ask their advice to smooth out the way before you.

Three mentors are ideal

From my years of experience coaching women, I've come to understand most women don't have enough outside support. As a working mother, I discovered I could only spend so much time nurturing mentoring relationships. Having ten mentors, for example, isn't realistic. But having only one mentor isn't ideal, either. Consider your three most important priorities where you'd benefit from guidance and support. Those are the areas in which mentors would be most helpful. Even if you want to take a single journey and there's one primary issue you want help with, having just one mentor isn't enough. One mentor alone can't give you a wide perspective of different viewpoints.

Acquiring three mentors is an unwritten rule based on my experience of busy women's lives and the challenges that may lie ahead for them. You can choose two mentors or four, but your choice should be based on what works best for you.

Change mentors as your needs change

As you grow, you'll need help with different things. When you're further along, it may be time to take a fresh look at the mentors you need at that stage in your career. You may still speak occasionally with your former mentors, but you might add another mentor when you need help with something different.

Return to the questions listed earlier and ask yourself, 'What do I need help with now?' Maybe it's a new skill such as presenting to or communicating with the board. Choose someone as a mentor with whom you feel a sense of chemistry, trust and a connection with the journey they've walked before you.

Make your mentoring request clear

Finding a mentor seems to happen organically and naturally when a younger man and an older man connect in the workplace. As a woman, it may not happen this way for you. In our new era of sensitivity regarding sexual misconduct and #metoo, senior men may be even less likely to proactively reach out to a young woman and say, 'I'm interested in helping you in your career. I see you're on the same track, the same journey I've been on. Would you like to set up a time for coffee?'

Since men may not be as likely to ask, you'll need to ask them. How do you do this? Before asking any questions at all, be sure you have trust and a connection with the person you want to mentor you. This means the first question you ask shouldn't be, 'Will you be my mentor?' Instead it should be, 'Could I ask your advice?' or, 'I have some questions I'd like to pose. Could we talk?' Build a relationship with your chosen mentor first.

When you ask for advice, you might say: 'I'm an Operations Specialist. You've walked the journey of VP of

Operations here. You've ... (and then list several of his or her achievements). I'd love to get your advice. Because I'd like to do that, too.'

Then have the conversation. Once you've sat down, be explicit. You might say: 'The reason I asked to have this conversation is because I'm focusing my career on advancing in operations, and I'd like your advice.' If you're comfortable and the conversation seems to go well, then use the word 'mentor'.

Say: 'This has been incredibly helpful for me. It's wonderful hearing from a person who's walked the journey. Would it be possible to meet again in the future, so I can ask you more questions? I'd love to learn more and have a mentor I can talk with.' Then it's clear how they can help you.

Senior-level people are busy. You don't walk up to a stranger and ask for an hour of their time, but fifteen to twenty minutes could be manageable. Be organised with your questions. You can always meet again if it's a productive conversation.

Don't take it personally if someone turns down your request for mentoring. They may simply be too busy, especially if they already have other mentees. Any mentor worth their salt will take their responsibility seriously and won't take you on if they know they can't commit the time.

Make your mentoring relationship win–win

Every relationship should be win–win, where both parties bring something positive to the equation. A mentor will appreciate it if there is something positive for him or her as well. Your mentor won't necessarily expect you to give them advice. At its purest, they may expect you to bring energy, enthusiasm, pertinent questions and a genuine hunger to learn. This should be enough reward for an executive interested in developing talent and building their legacy.

When you reach a senior position in an organisation, you become more focused on the larger needs of the firm. Developing potential leaders and building the organisation matters. For all the potential mentors you're asking to meet or share coffee with, someone helped them decades ago in their career. Or, someone asked them for coffee and advice and they benefited. Now, it's their turn to pass on the favour.

Think about what you can bring to the table in your mentoring relationships. You'll bring a different perspective based on the people you meet. Senior leaders often end up isolated in their world so you might be able to introduce them to a talented person with a different point of view.

Mentors genuinely appreciate your follow-up. If a senior executive spends valuable time with you and then never hears back from you, the circle is incomplete. But if you thank them in an email and say, 'Thank you for your time. I appreciate it. I used your idea and here's how it's working out,' then the relationship feels more two-way.

In addition to a thank you, perhaps you could add, 'I saw this article, and thought you might be interested.' Three months later, you could circle back and say, 'Thank you so much for the tool/book/suggestion we discussed. It's been a breakthrough for me. I've finished working through it and would love your advice on how to take it to the next level. Could we meet again? I'd appreciate hearing your thoughts.' That way you'll continue to benefit from the relationship you've built.

Everyone likes being asked for advice because they enjoy helping and knowing they're making a difference. Demonstrate that you listened, engaged with their advice and acted on it, and they'll be delighted they've made a difference and will be more inclined to meet with you to help you again.

Earn the respect of sponsors

Mentors are helpful, but over time, sponsors are more beneficial. In her 2013 book, *Forget a Mentor, Find a Sponsor,* author Sylvia Ann Hewlett writes:

'I thought that it was all about doing my job extraordinarily well. If I put my head down

and worked as hard as I knew how, my value
to the organisation would be self-evident,
and, of course, I would be recognised and
promoted.'

She was in the same circumstances as I was in. I found
sponsorship among my previous bosses, but then many
left the organisation. It wasn't until I focused on cul-
tivating a wider array of mentors and sponsors that I
got the support I needed to break through. Like most
women, I was raised to wait for people to notice me.
That simply doesn't bring results in corporate life.

Hewlett continues:

'Research we conducted at the Center for
Talent Innovation (CTI) shows that sponsors,
not mentors, give you real career traction and
put you on the path to power and influence by
affecting three things: pay raises, high-profile
assignments and promotions.'

The CTI research shows that individuals who are most
satisfied with their rate of advancement are individuals
with sponsors. They found 70 percent of sponsored
men and 68 percent of sponsored women feel they
are progressing through the ranks at a satisfactory
pace, compared to 57 percent of their peers who were
unsponsored.

You earn sponsorship. Once you, the quality of your
work, and your aspirations become known, senior

leaders may choose to become your sponsor. If they know you're enthusiastic about moving to another department or city for example, it's on their radar. If they believe in you, when a position comes up, they'll be likely to suggest you. There must be a trusting relationship and proof you'll do exceedingly well in whatever they advocate for you to take on. They must also understand your aspirations and goals before they can effectively advocate for you.

Who do *you* sponsor? Who do you advocate for when they aren't in the room? If you are at those meetings where candidates for a promotion or a new role are being discussed, speak up for women whose work you rate. If there are women not on the shortlists despite being a good match, query it. Be the change that you want to see.

Build a personal board of directors

In addition to mentors and sponsors at work, a personal board of directors is important to building your career. Consider your own career as a small business separate from where you work. For example, Helen Appleby LLC is a company. Build a board as you'd build a board for a company, like PepsiCo® or Apple®. Develop a list of informal, trusted advisors for your personal board of directors. These are the people who may be able to help with the major decisions in your life in the broadest sense, not just in your career. Consider all the functions of your life including legal, finance and Human Resources. Often people include their parents on their board of directors as well.

You may go to the same person on your board for relationship advice as you do for how much money you should put in your pension. Should I move to a new house? Should I rent or buy? Other decisions are likely to be asked of different people. Ask and consult with people on your journey like you'd consult with a board if you were a CEO.

It's highly unlikely there's a problem in the world that hasn't been solved already. Most problems with a human dimension have been solved before. We naturally think we must figure out everything ourselves, but we don't need to. Your personal board of directors can help you gain the perspective and experience of others.

Board members help you think on a broader scale. It's not just about the specific journeys you want to go on, it's about having access to wise people who can help you with big decisions. Just as a corporation considers diversity on their boards, think about the different skills on your board, too. Do you have:

- Someone who understands money?
- Someone who can help you with personal relationships?
- Someone who understands legal questions?

- Someone younger?

- Someone older?

- Someone who loves you unconditionally?

- Someone who'll challenge you to be and do more?

Write out a list of your personal board of directors. Make your list diverse as you consider life's problems and major decisions.

Your mentors, sponsors, and board of directors are the people who can guide and direct you through life and your career. They'll help you solve thorny problems, look out for possible landmines, and provide wise guidance and counsel you may not have considered. You don't have to resolve every problem on your own. Many people are capable and would be delighted to help you through the pitfalls and the peaks when you have questions or simply need to know which step to take next. And don't forget to pay this forwards by doing your part to support your sisterhood when you can too.

TWELVE

Sexual Harassment

One-third of women experience sexual harassment at least once in their career, according to the results of a 2015 survey in Cosmopolitan magazine.

Gretchen Carlson, a leading anchor for Fox News, endured years of sexual harassment at the hands of Chairman and CEO Roger Ailes. There were no checks and balances so that employees of Fox could feel respected or even safe at work. The organisation was rife with sexual harassment and assault which finally came to light when Carlson left and refused to go quietly. Some reports say the offices of the conservative news organisation were like a perpetual fraternity party. After more than a decade, she finally broke her silence. In 2016, she sued Ailes and won. Her book, *Be Fierce,* is a powerful declaration about how women can protect themselves from sexual harassment at work and regain their power against those who are abusers at the office.

Of course, famous women aren't the only ones who experience sexual harassment and assault. The focus on #metoo after the Weinstein scandal in 2017 has revealed it's a problem that millions of women struggle with at work. Until recently, women had stayed silent, sometimes even blaming themselves for the perpetrators' completely inappropriate behaviour. But when millions of women posted #metoo on social media platforms to show men how pervasive the problem is, a movement was born.

A 2018 study directed by the Society for Human Resources revealed that 62% of employers in the United States now provide workers with training programmes that tackle the matter of helping employees understand gender discrimination and sexual harassment at work. Another 94% have sexual harassment guidelines in place to protect employees from malicious conduct.

But don't let your guard down now that sexual misconduct is out in the open. The problem continues to fester. Yes, a few women who worked for high-profile bosses have had their day in court and prevailed. However, it's a mistake to think harassers have gone into hiding and will never strike again at work. Most women who experience this kind of abuse unfortunately never speak up and end up walking away from their job and their industry, while the abuser carries on their career with no consequences.

If you're dealing with a harasser, I've provided some common-sense unwritten rules which have proven highly effective. I'm obviously not an attorney and this chapter isn't intended to be legal advice. I'm based in the US now so the approach below is US-orientated but the laws are different in every country and in the US they also vary by state so check the legal situation in your country or state and in your company carefully first if you are dealing with an issue. Using these strategies will increase your chances of continuing in your job and focusing on your work without anxiety about being treated inappropriately. Keep in mind that silence rarely results in a harasser backing down. This isn't an easy road, but there are strategies.

According to the Society for Human Resources Management, 84% of people who engage in sexual misconduct are men. Only 16% are women. For that reason, I'll refer to abusers as 'he' and 'him', while acknowledging that's not always the case.

Know it's not your fault

Millions of women who are harassed at work blame themselves for this inappropriate behaviour. They suffer in silence and assume they must either put up with it or leave their job. In fact, the Society of Human

Resources Management estimates two out of three cases of all misconduct go unreported. The Equal Employment Opportunity Commission says that up to 75% of cases of harassment don't get reported. If you are suffering, you're probably not the only one. He's probably treating other women in your workplace abusively, too.

It's not your fault. The behaviour is called 'sexual misconduct', but it's not only about that. It's also about power and hostility, and is intended to make women feel intimidated, overwhelmed, and anxious.

Know your company policy before acting

If you've been affected by harassment, before you consider taking any action, know the policy your company uses for handling sexual misconduct. I realise it's upsetting, but educate yourself first. You may have signed paperwork when you started working there that says that, before you can go to a lawyer or government agency, you're required to go through a process of 'forced arbitration'. This would mean the company insists upon handling the situation internally. If that happens, you may end up having to leave your job and you may receive a settlement. You may also be required to sign a Non-Disclosure Agreement, effectively a gag order to prevent you from speaking publicly about what happened.

I was shocked when I discovered that in the US, small companies with fewer than fifteen employees aren't covered by the Civil Rights Act of 1964 which legislates for sexual misconduct at work. If you work for a small business, whether you have any legal protection or not is dependent on whether your state has laws protecting you.

If you go to Human Resources, you may set into motion a whole set of actions you're not ready for yet. Many Human Resources departments genuinely care about their employees having a safe, respectful environment to work in, because the people at the top care. However, some aren't as helpful because the people at the top haven't provided clear, strongly enforceable guidelines with a no tolerance policy for sexual misconduct. Some harassers are incredibly high performers and senior people themselves so Human Resources might be afraid for their own jobs if they blow the whistle.

You may wish to bring a complaint to the Equal Employment Opportunity Commission (EEOC) but you must first follow your company policy, or they won't allow you to proceed. If you follow your company policy with no results, then you can escalate to the EEOC.

There's a statute of limitations if you bring a case to the EEOC. This means you must file within 180 days in some instances. Once you make a complaint with the EEOC, they investigate and send you a reply stating whether you have the right to sue. You must then file suit within 90 days. Before filing, keep in mind that only 6% of cases ever go to trial, and only 2% prevail in court.

You may feel your only options are to remain silent, complain to Human Resources, or leave your job. But there's more you can do. For that reason, the remainder of the unwritten rules below are actions you can take to address the inappropriate behaviour without going to Human Resources. These are effective action steps which can result in the offending person realising his actions have no place at work.

Tell people you trust

I know that being a victim of sexual misconduct is isolating, lonely and difficult to cope with on your own. Most women think they're the only one being targeted. Usually it's not true. If it's happening to you, be careful to tell someone you trust. You need a support system, so you don't have to bear the load by yourself. Generally, telling people outside the company is the most prudent course, to avoid information getting back to the harasser. He may retaliate if he thinks you're spreading rumours.

According to an Associated Press-NORC Center for Public Affairs Research poll conducted in 2017, among those who've personally experienced sexual misconduct in the workplace, 83% said they feel angry about the experience. Most also agreed they felt humiliated and intimidated, and 48% said they feel ashamed about being mistreated. If you're a victim, don't go it alone.

Share your experience and feelings with someone who can support you.

Speak up at offensive behaviour.

Research indicates that ignoring inappropriate behaviour and hoping it'll go away without speaking up is ineffective. In Carlson's book, *Be Fierce,* one step she suggests is to openly take offence at offensive behaviour. When someone says something, does something, touches you inappropriately or worse, let it be known that what they're doing isn't welcome. You may cringe at the thought of it, but if you suffer in silence, the harasser may perceive that as acceptance that his behaviour is OK, or even welcome. A short, confident statement may put him in his place and stop it fast. Carlson suggests saying things like:

- 'Yes, I am offended. That's harassment.'

- 'My name is Karen. Please don't call me "honey".'

- 'That makes me uncomfortable.'

- 'I'm not interested in dating you. Don't ask me again.'

- 'Stop touching me.'

- 'Back off. That wasn't funny.'

- 'You're in my space. Step away.'

- 'Don't rub my shoulders. That's offensive.'

- 'Don't ever speak to me that way again.'

- 'You need to leave. You're embarrassing yourself.'

- 'That's harassment.'

Document everything that occurs

Documentation is essential if you decide to report a situation. Every time you have an encounter with a harasser that's clearly misconduct and makes you feel uncomfortable, write it down. Document the date it happened, where it happened, what happened, who else was in the room, what was said, and any other details in a journal or on your personal computer. Do it right away, so you remember everything. A journal can be a powerful tool if you ever decide to go to Human Resources, a lawyer, or a government agency. If you notice any retaliatory behaviour, document that as well. The Equal Employment Opportunity Commission released a comprehensive study in 2016 which said 75% of women who speak up experience retaliatory action from their harasser.

In our world of technology, another way to document everything is to record it. A recording provides proof that a conversation took place. We all have smart-phones with recording devices we could use. Keep in mind the rules for recording. In most instances in the

US, you can legally record a conversation if one person (you) knows it's happening. In eleven states, it's illegal to make a recording without the consent of all parties. You shouldn't record a conversation when you're not present. This means you can't turn a recorder on, leave the room and record a conversation in your absence.

In some cases, it's legal to record, but it's not admissible as evidence in court. But you could still play it to Human Resources. Remember, any editing of a recording isn't permitted. Be sure you understand your state and company policy before clicking the 'record' button.

Consider sending an email to the harasser

When a harasser won't take your short commands to heart, it may be time to send him an email, to provide deeper details about the issue and the change you want in clear terms.

This approach is suggested by Dr Bernice Sandler and was invented by Dr Mary Rowe at the Massachusetts Institute of Technology as a highly effective way of addressing his actions. If the harasser is unaware as to how his behaviour has impacted you, this email will give him the opportunity to see and understand his actions from your perspective. It will provide an emotionally compelling warning without publicly shaming or embarrassing him, which could result in retaliation. According to Sandler, the usual result is that the behaviour stops without further conversation. He suggests your email should be written in three factual, detailed parts:

- Part 1: State what happened. Include when it happened, where it happened, what took place, and who else was present. Be specific as you write. If the behaviour has happened several times, include as many instances as you can.

- Part 2: State how his words or actions made you feel and what the impact has been on you. This is the part of the letter where you should express your emotions, such as, 'Your behaviour makes me feel uncomfortable and intimidated.' Express if you've experienced any physical reaction before, during or after, too. If your stomach gets tied up in knots every time he walks into your office, say so. Don't let your anger or frustration get out of control, but use emotional words: intimidated, uncomfortable, trapped, dehumanised, cornered, embarrassed.

- Part 3: State what you want the harasser to do in clear terms. Give the parameters of what you want his behaviour to be going forward. You might say something like, 'I insist our working relationship be on a purely professional level.' Or, 'I want you to...'

An email will give him a chance to privately reconcile his behaviour with how it's impacted you and think about it without direct confrontation. He may not have a conversation with you about it but if the behaviour stops, you'll have achieved your objective. Remember to keep a hard copy of the email as a record.

Consider conducting a survey

The *New York Times* reported on how Women at Nike® did exactly this. In April 2018, women at Nike® finally decided something had to be done about the deeply misogynist culture there, but their laments to Human Resources went unheeded. In fact, Human Resources committed the unforgivable sin of telling women they were the source of the problem.

The scope of the unfair, unfriendly behaviour toward women went beyond sexual misconduct. Talented women were being passed over for promotion by less experienced men. Realising the need to support each other, the women banded together and conducted a simple survey to reveal the unsavoury truth. The survey results were delivered to the CEO's desk with a letter asking, 'Now, what are you going to do?'

Within a few weeks, six executives and sexual harassers had left the company. A month later, another wave of five executives left.

The survey worked for a few reasons:

- When people with complaints come together, they are no longer isolated. Companies that tolerate abuse will often tell the abused person that they're the only person who's complained. A survey with numerous women reporting the same problem proves the harassment is no isolated incident.

- Surveys provide data which is harder to ignore than one complaint at a time. In our respect for data, it's become more credible than individual reports.

- A survey is newsworthy and may garner unflattering headlines if it's leaked to the media. It could even go viral and no corporation wants unflattering publicity.

Because of the survey, Nike® let go of the most flagrant offenders who abused women in the workplace. They're also working to change the culture to one that seeks to level the playing field, which respects and rewards the contributions of women.

There is power in numbers. If you don't want to go it alone, you could uncover other women struggling with the same misconduct. Observe how other women react when they're around a harasser. Do they appear uncomfortable? Talk to a few people you trust and quietly ask around. As a group, you may decide the best way to confront the problem is to do it together.

Consider confronting the harasser in an intervention

You may be able to gather a group of women experiencing abuse at the hands of one man and confront him head on.

When an organised group of women confront an abuser, it's known as an intervention. It's a powerful, frightening experience for the man. In her 1993 book, *Back Off: How to confront and stop sexual harassment and harassers*, Martha Langelan says men don't expect individual women to stand up and work together. They're dumbfounded when women act collectively because they believe women won't organise a group. It violates the sexual stereotypes about women being unreliable for each other and too fearful. This action can be alarming for an abuser when he's yanked out of the shadows and revealed in the cold light of day.

In an intervention, so many women may be present, it may be almost impossible for him to retaliate. This makes it an incredibly effective tool.

Consider consulting a lawyer

If you're unsure, a consultation with a lawyer will help you know your options and whether you have a case. To bring a lawsuit in the US, you must prove:

- The harassment was due to your gender
- The harassment was unwelcome
- The harassment was so severe or pervasive it would affect a reasonable person's ability to work
- The company knew about it and failed to act appropriately

This is the standard of proof which must be met to file suit. The bar is a difficult one to scale. Bear in mind that cases are likely to be determined by judges who are men – old, white men. A lawyer can tell you if you have a reasonable case.

Navigating the landmines of sexual harassment is challenging. Lawsuits are long and expensive, and companies have deep pockets. Start with the simplest way to make the offending behaviour stop. If you must, escalate things one step at a time. If a group of women have been denied action through the corporation's sexual misconduct policy, that's another instance where it may be time to enlist the services of a lawyer.

I'm a strong supporter of changes to the law to make Non Disclosure Agreements (NDAs), which act as gag orders, unenforceable and to end forced arbitration, which takes away a woman's right to act outside the company. The illegal behaviour of perpetrators of sexual misconduct should be punished. A woman who has been a victim of sexual misconduct shouldn't be forced to leave her job because her abuser wields more legal power. The situation is changing and improving, but there's still a long way to go.

THIRTEEN

Be Resilient And Stay The Course

I was talking with a friend about everything I've learned as I climbed the corporate ladder. She is a creative entrepreneur and hasn't experienced many of the slings and arrows of corporate life.

She asked, 'Helen, when I think about how hard you worked in the corporate environment for twenty-five years, and everything it took for you to rise up to become a Vice President when men were promoted past you in the early years, plus all the injustices you endured, was it was worth it?'

Without skipping a beat, I replied, 'Absolutely!'

When I think collectively about all the learning, growth and change I went through to eventually succeed, there's much to be said for resilience and sticking with it. Often what I needed to learn had little to do with my work – my work was strong. However, not perceiving and understanding the unwritten rules that I've shared in this book held me back in many ways. I was too much of this and not enough of that for years before I figured it all out. Finally, I gained the wisdom and experience to succeed and prove conclusively these rules do work.

As I learned the rules and applied them to my career, it was as if the rain clouds floated away. Opportunities for increased responsibility and promotions came my way. I relished them, jumped in, and grew even more. Once I started my own business, I couldn't wait to share *The Unwritten Rules for Women's Leadership* with you.

I hope this chapter helps reassure you that despite the challenges, it's worth it. Yes, it's hard work. Success requires what often seems like endless hard work. There may be moments when you're so frustrated you want to pull your hair out or scream in the car while driving home. But I want to encourage you to stay the course. It's not just about knowledge of your field or your industry, but also about best practice for dealing with people, which I'm confident makes a massive difference.

Resilience is the ability to recover quickly from setbacks. In my career, some of those setbacks were short-term, for example, when a meeting went badly, or when I sat through a review where I was given information that I had no idea how to assimilate. There were times when I had impossible bosses, or was handed an enormous workload.

In a 2016 *Harvard Business Review article* entitled, 'Resilience is About How You Recharge, Not How You Endure' by Achor and Gielan, the authors say most of us have a misunderstanding of what it means to be resilient, and the impact of overworking: 'We often take a militaristic, "tough" approach to resilience and grit... We believe the longer we tough it out, the tougher we are, therefore the more successful we'll be. However, the science says this concept is inaccurate.'

The lack of a recovery period dramatically holds back our ability to be resilient and successful.

Practise self-care during and after the storms

Remember to practise self-care as you go through the storms of your career and your life. Work has certain storms, just like the weather. Over a longer period, there are times when the clouds part and work is calm again. Do your best to make it through each storm and practise as much self-care as you can. Self-care will help you recharge your batteries. Continue as much of your normal routine as possible while focusing on self-care, because it helps you make it through the storm.

When the storm ends and you have a period of calm, focus on your recovery from the onslaught. Treat yourself by getting extra sleep or extra exercise. Remember to take your annual leave. Return to your good habits again if you neglected your diet or routines during the storm.

In his book, *The Corporate Athlete,* Jack Groppel explains that being at work is like being an athlete. We're performers who must show up every day and compete. But our corporate careers are longer than an athlete's career – most athletes only compete until they're about thirty years old. In corporate life, we compete until we're sixty or sixty-five years old, sometimes even longer. For corporate athletes, there is no off-season.

Athletes build and sustain their ability to perform while maintaining their energy, both physical and emotional. After the big game, or at the end of the season, they build in as much recovery time as possible before performing and competing again. One course I took helped me finally understand what a difference getting enough sleep made to my performance.

Resilience is in recovery. It's about how we recharge our batteries. It's not about endurance. As human beings we aren't machines, and even machines require maintenance. We change the oil in our cars, check the tyre pressure, and take the car for a service if it starts to squeak or rattle. When our body squeaks, we should listen to it, too, and take steps to make it better.

Control what you can control

When I coach my clients about resilience in their lives, I tell them: 'Inevitably there will be ridiculously busy times. Sometimes you can't control the pace and the demands of work.' But even when you're going through a stressful period at work, there are facets of your life you can control. They may seem small, but in the grand scheme of things, they're incredibly important. It sounds obvious, but getting enough sleep, staying hydrated, eating healthy food, exercising, and perhaps meditating are important acts that we can control and which contribute to our self-care and resilience.

Meditation has become vital to me being ready to handle everything I must do for the day. I meditate for at least ten to fifteen minutes in the morning. It's a daily reminder to return to a place of calm. When I finish, I feel clear and ready to begin my day.

Back when I started my meditation practice, I thought you had to sit on the floor or on a yoga mat and listen to a guided meditation recording. Over time, I realised you can have a micro-meditation at your desk. You can meditate almost anywhere, and it will prove beneficial. We all do a reset or reboot on our computers from time to time. A micro-meditation only takes a minute or two. I once read, 'If you have time for Facebook, you certainly have time to meditate.'

Sometimes I'll arrive at a client's office, and if the traffic was horrible, and I feel out of sorts, I'll park my car and sit quietly for two minutes. I'll close my eyes and focus on my breath. Slowing down my thoughts as I count each breath helps clear my head and get me ready for what I'm doing next. I find it amazingly helpful.

Another way to feel centred and grounded, almost like a meditation, is to get out in nature. Step outside, or step away from your desk. If you can, go for a five-minute walk. Nature is the ideal environment for clearing your head.

Remind yourself how far you've come

If, in the middle of a storm, someone makes a nasty comment, or a meeting goes awry, take a moment to look inside. Remember how far you've come. Look back at your achievements. Reach inside and say, 'I'm good at this and I have value to add.'

Sometimes on rough days, I'll re-read the cards and notes in my Success File and remind myself I've done good work, I've made a difference and I should stay the course. Your own Success File will provide you with sustenance at times and a wonderful lift in those moments when you need it most.

Adapt and learn

Another part of resilience and staying the course is to look at how you can adapt and learn. Even if someone makes a nasty remark, try to ignore how they said it and think about what they said. Was there any truth in it? Is there something you can learn from it?

Occasionally I was put on projects for which I didn't have the skills. I was determined to succeed, yet I was totally out of my comfort zone. The worst time was when I was given a role that was a mixture of sales and auditing when my background was in marketing. I didn't possess the skills for the job and I thought my boss had set me up to fail. I asked for help, which was something I hadn't done earlier in my career. I reached out within the organisation. I even asked my dad, who was an accountant, for help. Don't suffer in silence. Remember, when things are the toughest, that's when you learn the most.

I got through this ordeal by asking:

- How do I ask for help, so I can do this?

- How do I try to adapt to this situation?

- How do I learn what I need to learn?

Later, in my final exit interview, my boss shocked me when he said, 'You're amazing and adaptable. I'd absolutely hire you again. I see such potential in you.'

I was stunned. There were times in that situation when I wouldn't have been surprised if he had fired me. We ended up friends.

Remember to be grateful

In the midst of the storm, remember what you have to be grateful for as you learn. Gratitude is enormously helpful. Even if it's tough, our lives in the corporate world are still privileged. Look at it from that perspective. A problem with your PowerPoint slides may be annoying, but it pales in comparison to what others are enduring in your city or around the world. Many people would happily trade places. Remember, you're learning and you're fortunate to be where you are compared to so many.

Do your best to start each day with a fresh, positive mindset. Think: 'Today is another lovely day. What am I grateful for?' A simple statement like this will help you create a better day. If you go to work with an attitude of, 'Today will be terrible', you'll subconsciously look for terrible things and find them. Instead, say, 'Today is a wonderful day!' and look for what's wonderful. It might be something simple, like the soup being delicious at lunch.

Keeping a balanced, healthy perspective also means not taking anything too seriously. Sometimes my team would say things like, 'It's only PowerPoint slides.'

Then someone would add, 'Nobody died.' A friend of mine says, 'We're not doing brain surgery.' At the end of the day, it's not that serious. This too shall pass, and life will go on.

Forgive yourself and others

What resonates with me most about forgiveness is that it's not so much about releasing mistakes, but bouncing back after the struggle. My worst days are when people are difficult, unreasonable, rude, or they shout. I don't mind people saying tough things, but I struggle when they say it in a hostile way. There's a distinction between saying difficult things and saying them in a way that's mean or rude.

When someone is in a bad mood, you have no idea what battles they're fighting. They could have a sick child. Their boiler could have exploded that morning. Perhaps they're still struggling with trauma from their childhood. Maybe they're sleep-deprived because they have a new baby. Who knows what could be going on?

In corporate life, few people are unpleasant on purpose. Most come to work to do a good job. They're not trying to make others miserable. Remembering that helps me depersonalise situations when people are difficult and bounce back from short-term difficulties. In uncomfortable moments, I'll think, 'Gee, I guess she didn't get any sleep last night.'

Remember your purpose

For me, making an impact and helping others keeps me going. I worked for a pharmaceutical company, and on a deeper level I always felt fulfilled when I remembered my larger purpose was helping people. When you have a sense you're doing good in the world, that knowledge can guide you on challenging days. Always stay connected to your personal purpose and its impact.

One classic book to help put your life in perspective is Viktor Frankl's *Man's Search for Meaning*. A concentration camp survivor, Frankl observed that the people who survived and made it out seemed to have a purpose that sustained them. They knew what they wanted to do with their lives after the war.

If you're feeling low, or you're having a tough day, one of the best things you can do to lift your mood is to think of something you can do for another person. Write a friendly card, give a genuine compliment, or give someone a physical or a virtual hug. It's impossible to be kind to someone else without the good feelings coming right back to you. When kindness and love come back, it's hard to be sad, down or self-absorbed. Little gestures for others like buying a cup of coffee for the person behind you in line or sending an email telling a person how much you appreciate them will bring you happiness, which will help you through tough times.

Conclusion

Now you know my unwritten rules. There may be some directions that took you by surprise as you read. Other rules, you may have heard before. But perhaps you hadn't acted on them yet because you didn't know how. You may have been focusing on working exceedingly hard. Like me, you may have hoped people would notice your excellent work and see you as the ideal person for the next step up on your career ladder. I hope you're convinced by now that this is not enough: you and your achievements must be visible. There are career accelerators and career decelerators, and maximising the accelerators makes a huge difference. Understanding the rules and the best ways to implement them will help you stand in your power both to move up and to be perceived as moving up.

I'd like to encourage you to step outside what's always felt comfortable and safe for you. Growth is usually experienced by doing something new that we've never done before and something that makes us feel uncomfortable at first. But once you incorporate a rule successfully, you'll feel more at ease about using it.

The unwritten rules will help you navigate the career journeys you want to take to become a more powerful, effective leader. Are you ready to:

- Move up in the Mood Elevator and return to 'curious' when you feel upset?

- Be more powerful and confident in meetings?

- Purposefully develop mentoring and sponsoring relationships that will accelerate your progress?

- Handle difficult conversations?

- Create relationships with stakeholders so that they support your efforts?

Writing this book meant I had to dig into my toolbox of the rules I teach my clients. It meant dredging up some unpleasant memories. On these pages, I've shared the meetings gone bad, the cringeworthy moments, and the missed opportunities when I should have spoken up more powerfully. Yes, we'd rather forget those moments, but I wanted to share both the ups and downs of my corporate journey, because I want you to know it happens to all of us.

Those moments were less than auspicious and yet analysing them was what enabled me to succeed. Then

I could concentrate on helping career-focused women grow and forge their own path, to write their own rules and stake their claim.

The distinguished US Secretary of State Madeleine Albright once said, 'There is a special place in hell for women who don't help other women.' I agree wholeheartedly. For far too long, the support that men are in the habit of giving one another has been so taken for granted that it is invisible – institutional, even – and it's time to redress the balance. There are those who try to drive a wedge between women, and they like nothing better than to see a bit of a 'cat fight'. A show of female solidarity is the best and most powerful way to turn the tables.

There are endless ways of deploying this sisterhood of solidarity, from the formal routes of mentoring and sponsoring that I've described in the book, to more informal means, like networking, sharing opportunities, noticing when someone is under pressure and offering her a lifeline, and generally making sure that your female colleagues' abilities and achievements are being recognised and talked about.

The rules in this book are mine. They are the lessons I wish I had learned earlier. They come from research and reading, and from hours working with hundreds of women who are on individual journeys in their careers. The conversation continues in my online course, where you can take the lessons even deeper with a group of women who will support you and be your sisterhood on the journey. There is also the 'Unwritten Rules of Women's Leadership' podcast, where I have the privilege of interviewing amazing, successful women who have agreed to share the struggles that they had on their journeys, how they overcame them, and what they learned to help women like you on your own journey. If you would like to be on the podcast or know someone you think I should interview, please reach out.

Now that you've completed *The Unwritten Rules of Women's Leadership*, I would welcome hearing from you. How has the book helped you to see your career path differently? I'd especially love to know how applying the unwritten rules is helping you grow and take the adventurous career journeys you want to embark upon.

Afterword: Questions for Men Who Want to Help

The fact that you're reading this afterword says a lot about you. Presumably, if you didn't want to help you wouldn't be reading. Any man reading a chapter in a book on women's leadership probably isn't part of the problem!

Recently I gave a talk on 'The Unwritten Rules of Women's Leadership' and I was pleased to see about 25% of the audience members were men. During my talk, there was a moment to ask men who want to help a few simple, thoughtful questions. My hope is that those men, including you, will take a few proactive steps to give women the opportunities to be heard and promoted. These straightforward questions will guide men in how they can assist high-potential women who want to grow.

Women at work aren't damsels in distress who need to be rescued. But there may be ways you can be more consciously aware of the behaviours that give women a fair, equal shot to grow alongside their male counterparts. I hope these questions serve as a filter for what you do or don't do, and the comments you make or choose to avoid. Here are the questions for you to consider:

Do you unintentionally make inappropriate comments?

Actor and comedian Peter White said, 'I think the golden rule for men should be: If you're a man, don't say anything to a woman on the street you wouldn't want a man saying to you in prison.' While that 'rule' may make you laugh, there is a stark kernel of truth in it. When a woman is with a man who's her senior, he may be larger in stature, but more importantly, he wields more power in the organisation.

Would you want to be in prison with a large man commenting to you about how nice your legs look? Or, how cute your outfit is?

This illustrates the inherent power differences between men and women. When you add the size difference to the power disparity, you come to understand how imperative it is to tread mindfully in your conversations.

Remember that what you can comfortably say to a friend, the wife of a friend, or your sister isn't perceived in the same way at work. Saying, 'That dress looks nice on you,' or, 'You look slim in that outfit,' may be appropriate when said to your sister or sister-in-law, because she's on the same level as you. But don't make a comment like that at work.

Hold yourself to a different standard in the workplace. When you talk with a woman at work, there's a hierarchy and you may be more senior than her. There is a power disparity in a work relationship not present in a family relationship or friendship where everyone is on equal footing.

Are you a leader you'd want your daughter to work for?

Why or why not? The leader you'd want your daughter to work for is a person who at the least allows her to feel safe and respected in the workplace. This means she doesn't feel like she needs to duck away or avoid being alone with him.

Look at your organisation or your team from the perspective of equality for both genders:

- Are 50% of your team members female at every level?

- Have you hired and promoted a diverse team?

- Are women paid equally for equal work? Do you know that?

- Do you consider the culture in your organisation or on your team friendly and safe for everyone?

- Do you have clear, strong sexual harassment policies in place?

- Do you provide the kind of work–life balance you'd like your daughter to have?

- Would she feel safe if she came to work with your organisation?

- If the answer to any of these questions is 'no', why not?

If you're not a CEO, you may not be able to change the entire company. However, you could make your department or team a great place for women to work. You could adjust policies and procedures so both women and men feel comfortable and know there are truly equal opportunities for growth.

Do you listen carefully?

Most people believe they listen, but often they listen just long enough to find a break in what a woman says so they can interrupt. This is the experience of many women, including senior women. Do you listen for where the idea originated? Or, do you only listen to the loudest voice in the room?

"That's an excellent suggestion, Miss Triggs. Perhaps one of the men here would like to make it."

The statement depicted in the cartoon above is the experience I hear constantly from women. Even senior women experience this at work. It happened to me numerous times as a Vice President. A senior woman I knew who was a divisional president of her company had her ideas stolen by a man junior to her.

Are you interrupting?

For some reason, men often think women do all the talking. This is not backed up by research. Why do men perceive women as the ones talking all the time? Traditional gender roles demand women should be listeners and not speakers, so a woman who speaks as much as a man comes across as talking 'too much'.

A 2014 study conducted by Kieran Snyder revealed men interrupt a person speaking in a meeting twice as often as women do. When men interrupt, they're three times more likely to interrupt a woman. This phenomenon has been dubbed 'manterrupting'.

Researcher Dale Spender of Australia used audio and video to independently evaluate who talked most in mixed-gender university classroom discussions. Regardless of the gender ratio of students, whether the instructor deliberately tried to encourage female participation or not, men *always* talked more, whether the metric was minutes of talking or the number of words spoken.

When Spender asked students to evaluate their perception of who talked more, women were accurate. Men perceived the discussion as being 'equal' when women talked *only 15% of the time. They felt* the discussion was dominated by women if they talked *30% of the time.* These findings were reported in Spender's 1980 book, *Learning to Lose: Sexism and Education.*

Deborah Tannen, Professor of Linguistics at Georgetown and bestselling author of *You Just Don't Understand: Men and Women in Conversation,* says:

'Women and men have different speaking
styles: women listen more and expect a certain

intimacy. Men, by contrast, are more direct and especially in the workplace speak in ways to, "Position themselves as one up." Men tend to be competitors and women are connectors.'

Do you hold women to a different standard?

Women are judged harshly. Either they are too feminine and weak, or too masculine and strident. This makes it difficult for a woman to strike a balance that helps her to be heard and to be promoted. When you say a woman is 'too ambitious' or 'too aggressive', are you judging them the same way as you judge a man? Women tend to walk tightropes of acceptable behaviour that are much narrower than men's.

In her book *Lean In*, Sheryl Sandberg cites an experiment conducted at Columbia Business School and New York University. They took a Harvard University case study of the resume of a real person who was a venture capitalist and a successful silicon valley entrepreneur and gave it to their classrooms of students. Half the class saw the resume with the name Heidi Rosen at the top. Without changing anything on the resume, the other half of the class was handed the same resume with the name Howard Rosen on it. They then asked the students to evaluate this entrepreneur on various attributes. Both were viewed as equally competent. Howard was considered likeable. Heidi was perceived as selfish and the type of person you wouldn't want to hire or have as a boss. The only thing changed on the resume was the name from Heidi to Howard.

I've already discussed research conducted by McKinsey and Hewlett Packard where men are given credit and promoted based on their unrealised 'potential', while women are promoted based on their proven track record.

Men are often uncomfortable about promoting a woman and taking a chance on her. After years of trying to achieve Vice President status with an excellent track record, I discuss earlier in this book that the man who finally promoted me said those exact words: 'No one's taken a chance on you.' It's unconscious behaviour, and both men and women do it, but that doesn't make it right.

Listen to yourself when you describe a woman of ambition determined to grow. Would you say the same thing if her name was Tom rather than Tina? Be aware of unfair judgements and stop holding women to different standards that leave them on the tightropes.

What standards do you hold other men to?

#Complicit was the word of the year in 2017. In the aftermath of Harvey Weinstein's dramatic fall and that of other powerful men, many who knew about their entirely inappropriate behaviour as sexual predators were left to consider what they could have done differently.

Ask and expect more of the men you work with. Men are complicit when they ignore the inappropriate behaviour of other men. Do you tolerate the bad behaviour of men you work with? What standard do you hold yourself to? What standards do you hold other men to?

Your words can have a huge impact on the men at work. Say words like:

- 'Let her finish.'
- 'That's not cool.'
- 'That's sexist.'
- 'That's not fair.'

These words can be powerful conversation changers. It's not about rescuing women. What matters is how much you can help when you see unconscious bias or outright sexism. Do you stand up and get in the way to make a difference? Or are you complicit and let it slide? Only you can answer that question.

Do you 'mansplain'?

Mansplaining happens when a man explains the blindingly obvious to a woman in a way that's downright insulting. A Finance Director more junior than me regularly took it upon himself to explain some of the most basic aspects of marketing to me in meetings. I was Global Vice President of Marketing at the time. Do you do that? Do you hear it happen in your meetings?

Will #metoo stop men from helping women?

The unintended consequence of the #metoo movement that concerns me is the likelihood that good, smart men who aren't sexual harassers or predators will be even more cautious about mentoring and sponsoring women, for fear of a backlash. They will be even less likely to take an active interest in women's careers and ask to spend time with them alone. If this happens, we will miss out on your experience and wisdom. We'll lose out on the guidance you might otherwise impart to us. Please engage and get involved in a way that's clear, appropriate and above board.

Who do you mentor?

We're all drawn to people like ourselves. It's natural to take an interest in someone who reminds us of ourselves. My experience with male senior management is that they often are unconsciously drawn to younger men they can mentor, confide in, hang out with and talk to about sports. They compare football scores and share a beer. I encourage you to make a list of who you take an interest in and who you spend time with. As you look over your list, you may realise you've only mentored men.

What would happen if you expanded that circle? Could you mentor more people who don't look like yourself? Could you mentor 50% women?

Your advice is incredibly helpful. If you genuinely want to help, then mentor women as well as men. It's important to do it properly. You can ask a high-potential woman if she'd like to be mentored. Do it in an appropriate way. Express clearly why you're taking an interest in her career. Give her some advice and let her know how you'd like to mentor her. Say it in a way that doesn't feel creepy or weird. You could say: 'I have some advice I feel will be helpful. Can we have lunch together?' or, 'I've heard you want to move into finance. Would you like to talk about it?'

Who do you sponsor?

Mentors are helpful at one level of changing the game. However, sponsorship is even more powerful. The people you sponsor are the ones you go to bat for. They're the ones you advocate for when they're not in the room. When you honestly say, 'Janet would be fantastic in that role', that's how you act as a sponsor.

Consider your list of people you're willing to advocate for when they're not in the room. Is your list a diverse one? Jot down why you're willing to help each one. What have they proven to you? What potential do they possess? Learn about the careers of others. Find a few who don't remind you of yourself and build relationships with them so you can advocate for them.

Are you amplifying women's voices?

A notoriously frustrating aspect of workplace sexism for women is being overlooked or ignored in meetings. When you amplify women's voices, if you repeat their idea, you credit the ones who came up with it. The net effect is that it forces men to acknowledge women's contribution to the conversation.

According to a Washington Post report, when President Obama took office, two thirds of his top aides were men, making it difficult for women to be heard and work their way into better positions. As more women made their way into important conversations, they used the strategy of 'amplification' to ensure their voices were heard. Former White House Senior Advisor Valerie Jarrett said, 'It certainly helped in the long run. There was a lot of testosterone flowing in those early days. Gradually a little more estrogen provided a counterbalance.'

Their dedication to amplifying each other's voices paid off. The women kept doing it purposefully, so it became an everyday occurrence in meetings. The President noticed and asked what they were doing. He joined in to help them be heard and started calling on and consulting more women staffers. Interestingly, he was a president who has two daughters. Some of our best advocates are men with daughters who are starting to consider their career choices.

If you genuinely want to help, these questions are easy to answer. If you haven't been doing it and have more to do, you may discover the answers are tougher.

References

Introduction – Why Do I Need Unwritten Rules?

Hinchcliffe, Emma, 'The Number of Female CEOs in the Fortune 500 Hits an All-Time Record', *Fortune*, 2020, https://fortune.com/2020/05/18/women-ceos-fortune-500-2020, accessed 30 August 2020.

Joshi, Aparna, Son, Jooyeon, and Roh, Hyuntak, 'When Can Women Close the Gap? A Meta-Analytic Test of Sex Differences in Performance and Rewards', *Academy of Management Journal*, 58/5 (2015), 1516–1545.

Lyons Cole, Lauren, 'There's a Reason the Highest-Paid Men in the US Earn More Than Women – But It's Not The Pay Gap', Business Insider, 2017, www.businessinsider.com/why-men-earn-more-than-women-2017-7, accessed 30 January 2020.

Sandberg, Daniel, 'When Women Lead, Firm Wins', S&P Global, 2019, www.spglobal.com/_division_assets/images/special-editorial/iif-2019/whenwomenlead_.pdf, accessed 30 August 2020.

Snyder, Kieran, 'How to Get Ahead as a Woman in Tech: Interrupt Men.' *Slate Magazine*, 2014, https://sites.psu.edu/siowfa16/2016/10/20/do-men-tend-to-interrupt-more-than-women, accessed 30 January 2020.

Sweeney, Deborah, 'It Takes Dedication, Not a Skirt or Pants, to Lead a Business to Success', Forbes.com, 2013, www.forbes.com/sites/deborahsweeney/2013/01/24/it-takes-dedication-not-a-skirt-or-pants-to-lead-a-business-to-success/#25bb65662c98, accessed 30 January 2020.

Thomas, Rachel et al, *Women in the Workplace*, McKinsey & Company and LeanIn.Org, 2019, https://womenintheworkplace.com, accessed 30 January 2020.

W.E., 'What's Holding Women Back?', *The Economist*, 2015, www.economist.com/democracy-in-america/2015/01/23/whats-holding-women-back, accessed 30 January 2020.

Williams, Joan C and Dempsey, Rachel (2014) *What Works for Women at Work*, NYU Press.

1 My Corporate Career Journey

Collins, Jim (2001) *Good to Great,* Harper Business.

Ely, Robin J, Stone, Pamela, and Ammerman, Colleen, 'Rethink What You "Know" About High-Achieving Women', *Harvard Business Review*, 2014, https://hbr.org /2014/12/rethink-what-you-know-about-high-achieving -women, accessed 30 January 2020.

Fels, Anna, 'Do Women Lack Ambition?', *Harvard Business Review*, 2004, https://hbr.org/2004/04/do -women-lack-ambition, accessed 30 January 2020.

Hideg, Ivona, 'Do Longer Maternity Leaves Hurt Women's Careers?', *Harvard Business Review*, 2018, https://hbr.org/2018/09/do-longer-maternity-leaves -hurt-womens-careers, accessed 30 August 2020.

Thomas, Rachel et al, *Women in the Workplace*, McKinsey & Co. and LeanIn.Org, 2019, https:// womenintheworkplace.com, accessed 30 January 2020.

McKinsey & Company, 'Unlocking The Full Potential of Women In The US Economy', *Wall Street Journal*, 2011, www.mckinsey.com/~/media/McKinsey/dotcom /client_service/Organization/PDFs/Exec_Summ_WSJ _Preview_Special_Report.ashx, accessed 30 August 2020.

2 Self-leadership

Dweck, Carol S (2007) *Mindset: The New Psychology of Success*, Ballantine Books.

Senn, Larry, *The Mood Elevator*, MoodElevator.com, https://themoodelevator.com, accessed 30 January 2020.

3 Confidence Management

Kumar, Shamala, and Jagacinski, Carolyn M, 'Imposters Have Goals Too: The Imposter Phenomenon and Its Relationship to Achievement Goal Theory', *Personality and Individual Differences*, 40/1 (2006), 147–157.

Murphy, Joseph (2011) *The Power of Your Subconscious Mind*, Martino Publishing.

4 Personal Branding

Annis, Barbara, Lawrence, Carolyn and Doerr, Patsy, *Women of Influence: Solutions to Women's Advancement*, Thomson Reuters, 2014, www.womenofinfluence.ca /wp-content/uploads/2014/04/Women-of-Influence -WhitePaper-2014.pdf, accessed 30 January 2020.

Schmidt, Carol, 'Study: Interventions Help Women's Reluctance to Discuss Accomplishments', Medical Press, 2014, https://medicalxpress.com/news/2014

-01-interventions-women-reluctance-discuss.html, accessed 30 January 2020.

Smith, Jessi L, and Huntoon, Meghan, 'Women's Bragging Rights', *Psychology of Women Quarterly*, 38/4 (2013), 447–459, https://www.researchgate.net/publication/270643008_Women's_Bragging_Rights, accessed 30 August 2020.

5 Self-promotion

Bowley, Rachel, 'Women's Equality Day: A Look at Women in the Workplace in 2017', LinkedIn.com, 2017, https://blog.linkedin.com/2017/august/28/womens-equality-day-a-look-at-women-in-the-workplace-in-2017, accessed 30 January 2020.

Coleman, Harvey (2010) *Empowering Yourself: The Organizational Game Revealed*, AuthorHouse.

League, Levo, 'Why Is Self-Promotion So Hard for Women?', *Forbes*, 2011, www.forbes.com/sites/levoleague/2011/12/02/why-is-self-promotion-so-hard-for-women/#28c4340b4816, accessed 30 January 2020.

McCormick, Horace, 'The Real Effects of Unconscious Bias in the Workplace', UNC Executive Development, 2016, http://execdev.kenan-flagler.unc.edu/the-real-effects-of-unconscious-bias-in-the-workplace-thank-you-0?submissionGuid=1ea4245b-044b-4140-adba-c5e400ae8536, accessed 30 January 2020.

Mohr, Tara (2015, reprint edition) *Playing Big: Practical Wisdom for Women Who Want to Speak Up, Create, and Lead*, Penguin Random House USA.

Rezvani, Selena (2012) *Pushback: How Smart Women Ask – and Stand Up – for What They Want*, Jossey-Bass.

Silva, Christine, 'The Myth of the Ideal Worker: Does doing all the right things really get women ahead?', Catalyst, 2011.

6 Leadership Presence and Impact

Brion, S, Moore, D A, and Kennedy, J A (2012) 'A status-enhancement account of overconfidence.' *Journal of Personality and Social Psychology*, 103(4), 718–735. https://doi.org/10.1037/a0029395, https://psycnet.apa.org/record/2012-18756-001, accessed 30 January 2020.

Cuddy, Amy (2015) *Presence: Bringing Your Boldest Self to Your Biggest Challenges*, Little, Brown Spark.

Fortier, Mark, 'New Study From the Center for Talent Innovation Reveals How to Get Promoted Now', Prweb, 2012, www.prweb.com/releases/2012/10/prweb10050433.htm, accessed 30 January 2020.

Hewlett, Sylvia Ann (2014) *Executive Presence: The Missing Link Between Merit and Success*, Harper Business.

Swanson, Ana, 'The Real Reason Women Take So Long Getting Ready', *Washington Post*, 2016, www .washingtonpost.com/news/wonk/wp/2016/05/19/the -real-reason-that-so-many-women-have-to-spend-so -much-time-getting-ready/?utm_term=.7581584160a9, accessed 30 January 2020.

7 Influencing Skills

Babcock, Linda, Laschever, Sara, Gelfand, Michele and Small, Deborah, 'Nice Girls Don't Ask', *Harvard Business Review*, 2003, https://hbr.org/2003/10/nice -girls-dont-ask, accessed 30 January 2020.

Bradford, David L and Cohen, Allan R (2004, 2nd edition) *Influence Without Authority*, John Wiley & Sons.

Goldsmith, Marshall (2008) *What Got You Here Won't Get You There*, Profile Books.

Veihmeyer, John, Doughtie, Lynne and Day-oan, Sharon, 'KPMG Women's Leadership Study: Moving Women Forward into Leadership Roles', KPMG, 2015, https://home.kpmg/content /dam/kpmg/ph/pdf/ThoughtLeadershipPublications /KPMGWomensLeadershipStudy.pdf, accessed 30 January 2020.

8 Difficult Conversations

Cooper, Marianne, 'For Women Leaders, Likability and Success Hardly Go Hand-In-Hand', *Harvard Business Review*, 2013, https://hbr.org/2013/04/for-women -leaders-likability-a, accessed 30 January 2020.

Cuddy, Amy (2016) *Presence: Bringing your boldest self to your biggest challenges,* Orion Books.

Gallo, Amy (2017) *HBR Guide to Dealing with Conflict,* Harvard Business Publishing.

Goldsmith, Marshall (2007) *What Got You Here Won't Get You There,* Profile Books.

Weiss, Avrum, *'Men's Anger Might Mask Fear'*, 2018, PsychologyToday.com, www.psychologytoday.com/us /blog/fear-intimacy/201809/mens-anger-might-mask -fear, accessed 30 January 2020.

9 Negotiating Strategies

Amanatullah, Emily T, and Morris, Michael W, 'Negotiating Gender Roles: Gender Differences in Assertive Negotiating Are Mediated by Women's Fear of Backlash and Attenuated When Negotiating on Behalf of Others', *Journal of Personality and Social Psychology*, 98/2 (2010), 256–267.

Babcock, Linda and Laschever, Sara (2008) *Ask for It: How Women Can Use the Power of Negotiation to Get What they Really Want*, Bantam.

Babcock, Linda and Laschever, Sara (2003) *Women Don't Ask: Negotiation and the gender divide*, Princeton University Press.

Bowles, Hannah Riley, Babcock, Linda, Lai, Lei, 'Social Incentives for Gender Differences in the Propensity to Initiate Negotiations: Sometimes it does hurt to ask', *Organizational Behavior and Human Decision Processes*, 2007, 103, 84–103.

Brzezinski, Mika (2011) *Knowing Your Value*, Hachette Books

Small, Deborah A, Gelfand, Michele, Babcock, Linda, and Gettman, Hilary, 'Who Goes to the Bargaining Table? The Influence of Gender and Framing on the Initiation of Negotiation', *Journal of Personality and Social Psychology*, 93/4 (2007), 600–613.

10 Work–life Balance

Arbor, Ann, 'Exactly How Much Housework Does a Husband Create?', *Michigan News*, University of Michigan, 2008, https://news.umich.edu/exactly-how-much-housework-does-a-husband-create, accessed 30 January 2020.

Barberio, Joseph, 'This Comic Perfectly Explains the Mental Load Working Mothers Bear', *Working Mother,* 2008, www.workingmother.com/this-comic-perfectly -explains-mental-load-working-mothers-bear, accessed 30 January 2020.

Coleman, Jackie and John, 'How Two-Career Couples Stay Happy', *Harvard Business Review*, 2012, https:// hbr.org/2012/07/how-two-career-couples-stay-happy, accessed 30 January 2020.

Edgell Becker, Penny, and Moen, Phyllis, 'Scaling Back: Dual-Earner Couples' Work-Family Strategies', *Journal of Marriage and Family* 61/4 (1999), 995-107.

Evans, Lisa, 'Are Kids of Working Mothers Better Prepared for Their Future Careers?', Fast Company, 2016, www.fastcompany.com/3055606/are-kids-of-working -moms-better-prepared-for-their-future-careers, accessed 30 January 2020.

Harvard Business School, 'Having A Working Mother is Good For You', 2015, https://www.hbs.edu/news /releases/Pages/having-working-mother.aspx, accessed 30 January 2020.

O'Connell, Andrew, 'The One Thing About Your Spouse's Personality That Really Affects Your Career', *Harvard Business Review*, 2015, https://hbr.org/2014/11 /the-one-thing-about-your-spouses-personality-that -affects-your-career, accessed 30 January 2020.

Valcour, Monique, 'Navigating Tradeoffs in a Dual Career Marriage', *Harvard Business Review*, 2015, https://hbr.org/2015/04/navigating-tradeoffs-in-a-dual-career-marriage, accessed 30 January 2020.

Women Returners, 'Research data summary – Career Breaks & Returning to Work', Women Returners Ltd, 2014, http://corp.womenreturners.com/research-data-summary, accessed 30 January 2020.

11 Mentors and Sponsors

Carlson, Gretchen (2017) *Be Fierce*, Center Street.

Drexler, Peggy, 'Can Women Succeed Without a Mentor?', *Forbes*, 2014, www.forbes.com/sites/peggydrexler/2014/03/04/can-women-succeed-without-a-mentor, accessed 30 January 2020.

Hewlett, Sylvia Ann (2013) *Forget a Mentor, Find a Sponsor*, Harvard Business Review Press.

McCormick, Horace, 'The Real Effects of Unconscious Bias in the Workplace', UNC Executive Development, 2016, http://execdev.kenan-flagler.unc.edu/the-real-effects-of-unconscious-bias-in-the-workplace-thank-you-0?submissionGuid=1ea4245b-044b-4140-adba-c5e400ae8536, accessed 30 January 2020.

Ragins, Belle Rose, and Cotton, John L, 'Easier Said Than Done: Gender differences in Perceived Barriers to Gaining a Mentor', *Academy of Management Journal*, 34/4 (1991), 939-951.

12 Sexual Harassment

Carlson, Gretchen (2017) *Be Fierce,* Center Street.

Cresswell, Julie et al, 'At Nike, Revolt Led By Women Leads to Exodus of Male Executives', *New York Times*, 2018, www.nytimes.com/2018/04/28/business/nike -women.html, accessed 30 January 2020.

Investigations Law Group, 'Retaliation Prevention Requires a Robust Policy and Proactive Process', 2019, www.lexology.com/library/detail.aspx?g=47194ed9 -ac9d-4fab-b9a9-1f05e74c6a9c, accessed 30 January 2020.

Langelan, Martha J (1993) *Back Off: How to Confront and Stop Sexual Harassment and Harassers,* Touchstone.

Ruiz, Michelle, and Ahn, Lauren, 'Survey: 1 in 3 Women Has Been Sexually Harassed at Work', *Cosmopolitan*, 2015, https://www.cosmopolitan.com/career /news/a36453/cosmopolitan-sexual-harassment-survey, accessed 30 January 2020.

Sandler, Bernice R, 'Intervening When You Observe Sexual Harassment of One Person By Another', National Association for Women In Education, 2003, www .whoi.edu/images/gepac/intervening.pdf, accessed 30 January 2020.

SHRM, 'Harrassment-Free Workplace Series: A Focus on Sexual Harrassment', 2018, www.shrm.org/hr-today /trends-and-forecasting/research-and-surveys/pages /a-focus-on-sexual-harassment.aspx, accessed August 30, 2020.

US Equal Employment Commission, 'Select Task Force on the Study of Harassment in the Workplace', 2016, www.eeoc.gov/select-task-force-study-harassment -workplace, accessed 30 January 2020.

Wilkie, Dana, 'When HR Gets It Wrong: Misconduct Won't Change Until the Culture Does', Society of Human Resource Management, 2017, www.shrm .org/resourcesandtools/hr-topics/employee-relations /pages/hr-gets-it-wrong-4-.aspx, accessed 30 January 2020.

13 Be Resilient and Stay the Course

Achor, Shawn and Gielan, Michelle, 'Resilience is About How You Recharge Not How You Endure', *Harvard Business Review*, 2016, https://hbr.org/2016/06/resilience-is-about-how-you-recharge-not-how-you-endure, accessed 30 January 2020.

Frankl, Victor (1946) *Man's Search for Meaning*, Beacon Press.

Groppel, Jack (1999) *The Corporate Athlete*, John Wiley & Sons.

Seldman, Marty and Seldman, Joshua (2008) *Executive Stamina*, John Wiley & Sons.

Sluiter, Judith K, 'The Influence of Work Characteristics on the Need for Recovery and Experienced Health: A Study on Coach Drivers', *Ergonomics 42/4 (1999)*, 573–583.

Werner, Emmy, 'Resilience and Recovery: Findings from the Kuai Longitudinal Study', *Research, Policy, and Practice in Children's Mental Health* 19/1 (2005), 11–14.

Afterword For Men Who Want to Help

Barsh, Joanna and Yee, Lareina, 'Unlocking the Full Potential of Women at Work', McKinsey & Company, 2012, www.mckinsey.com/business-functions /organization/our-insights/unlocking-the-full -potential-of-women-at-work, accessed 30 January 2020.

Dudding, Adam, 'Are Men Really Talking Too Much? We've Done the Maths', *Stuff*, 2017, www.stuff.co.nz /life-style/life/89851118/are-men-really-talking-too -much-weve-done-the-maths, accessed 30 January 2020.

Eilperin, Juliet, 'White House Women Want to be in the Room Where it Happens', *Washington Post*, 2016, www .washingtonpost.com/news/powerpost/wp/2016/09 /13/white-house-women-are-now-in-the-room-where -it-happens/?utm_term=.750713850ed2, accessed 30 January 2020.

Sandberg, Sheryl, and Grant, Adam, 'Speaking While Female', *New York Times*, 2015, www.nytimes.com/2015 /01/11/opinion/sunday/speaking-while-female.html, accessed 30 January 2020.

Snyder, Kieran, 'How to Get Ahead as a Woman in Tech: Interrupt Men', *Slate*, 2014, https://slate.com/human -interest/2014/07/study-men-interrupt-women-more -in-tech-workplaces-but-high-ranking-women-learn-to -interrupt.html, accessed 30 January 2020.

University of Sheffield, 'Male and Female Voices Affect Brain Differently', University of Sheffield, 2005, www .sheffield.ac.uk/news/nr/422-1.174743, accessed 30 January 2020.

Sandberg, Sheryl (2013) *Lean In: Women, work, and the will to lead*, Knopf.

Spender, Dale and Sarah, Elizabeth (1993, reprint edition) *Learning to Lose: Sexism and Education*, Women's Press Ltd.

Tannen, Deborah (1992) *You Just Don't Understand: Women and Men in Conversation*, Virago.

Acknowledgements

My dad passed away several years ago and my daughter Ellie is now twenty years old and in college. I want this book to make a difference for her, for you, and for all our daughters. Because I know my dad was right when he told me that 'girls can do anything boys can do', and I've never stopped thanking him for that.

'It takes a village' in life, in our careers, in raising children, in entrepreneurship and in writing a book. So, I'd like to thank the many great bosses that I had on my journey; Jill Winter, Caroline Whitfield, John Clark, Ian McPherson, Clive Addison, Paul Wheeler, Stan Lech, Anup Chib and Chris Rich really stand out and many are mentioned in the book.

My siblings – Claire, Bruce and Andrew, my global 'sisterhood' of supporters on the journey: Amy, Stef, Deb, Gayten, Gerilyn, Emma, Holly, Kelly, Helen, Natalie, Sabina, Clare, Donna, Jane, Renu and Bonnie to name just a few.

Huge thanks also to my 'Tribe' – Mike, Alex, Mark, Tony, Christina, JC, Nathan, Mandy, Vivian, Tom and others who have kept me sane on my entrepreneurial journey as well as Rich Litvin, Chris Smith, Denise Michaels, Toby Goodman, Daniel Priestley, and the team at Rethink Press who helped me give birth to my 'Book Baby' and kept me going when the impostor syndrome voices got loud!

My clients are a huge inspiration for me – you know who you are – and I kept writing for you when it got hard!

The Author

Helen Appleby is a US-based British executive coach, leadership trainer and podcaster who has a strong track record of leadership and commercial success.

She was previously a VP and Global Business Leader for GlaxoSmithKline where she led the $1bn Respiratory Health business in Consumer Healthcare. Her career at GSK and Unilever spanned six countries and she has lived and worked in Canada, UK, Cyprus, Dubai, Malaysia and the US. Her podcast is called 'The Unwritten Rules of Women's Leadership' and features successful women sharing their challenges and lessons of success.

She is the proud mum of Alex and Ellie, a fantastic shopper, an average yogi and a terrible cook.

⊕ www.theunwrittenrules.com
ⓘⓝ www.linkedin.com/in/helenappleby

Made in the USA
Columbia, SC
06 November 2020